DYLAN THOMAS

Before his tragic death at 39, Dylan Thomas was already recognized as the greatest lyric poet of the younger generation. Wide appreciation of his fiction and other prose writings has been largely posthumous.

Born in 1914 in the Welsh seaport of Swansea, he was early steeped in Welsh lore and poetry, and in the Bible, all of which left their mark on his rich, startling imagery and driving rhythms. As a boy, he said he "was small, thin, indecisively active, quick to get dirty, curly." His formal education ended with the Swansea Grammar school; and thereafter he was at various times a newspaper reporter, a "hack writer," an odd-job man, a documentary film scriptwriter.

The rich resonance of his "Welsh-singing" voice led to Dylan Thomas reading other poets' work as well as his own over the B.B.C. Third Programme. It also brought him to the United States, in 1950, '52 and '53, where he gave readings of his own and other poetry in as many as 40 university towns, and made three magnificent long-playing records published by Caedmon. "I don't believe in New York," he said, "but I love Third Avenue."

Since Dylan Thomas's death in 1953 his reputation and popularity have steadily increased. His poetry is studied in hundreds of American colleges, and his prose books such as *Adventures in the Skin Trade, Portrait of the Artist as a Young Dog, Quite Early one Morning* and *A Child's Christmas in Wales* are paperback bestsellers. Many books have been written about his life and work, while a play about him, in which Alec Guinness portrayed Dylan, was a Broadway hit.

In 1967 New Directions published *Selected Letters*, edited by Constantine FitzGibbon, and Thomas's *Notebooks* of the period 1930-34, edited by Ralph Maud, containing drafts of some 200 poems, most of them previously unpublished. *Rebecca's Daughters*, a film scenario of a romantic adventure story set in the mid nineteenth-century Wales, was published in 1982. *On the Air with Dylan Thomas*, a collection of all of Thomas's BBC radio work excepting *Under Milkwood* was published in 1992.

QUITE EARLY ONE MORNING

BY DYLAN THOMAS

Dylan Thomas

Quite Early One Morning

A New Directions Paperbook

Library of Congress Catalog Card Number: 54-12907

ISBN: 0-8112-0208-9

Manufactured in the United States of America.
New Directions books are printed on acid-free paper.
Published in Canada by Penguin Books Canada Limited.

New Directions Books are published for James Laughlin
by New Directions Publishing Corporation,
80 Eighth Avenue, New York 10011

TWENTIETH PRINTING

CONTENTS

PUBLISHER'S NOTE

The stories and essays here assembled for the first time were written over a period of some ten years: the latest, "A Visit to America," was read by Dylan Thomas on his last tour of the United States in 1953. Shortly before his sudden illness and death, Thomas sketched out plans for such a volume of prose pieces to be called "Quite Early One Morning." Since so many of the pieces he wanted to include had been commissioned by the British Broadcasting Corporation, his literary executors and the trustees of his estate asked Mr. Aneirin Talfan Davies, Director of the Welsh Region, B.B.C., who had worked closely with Thomas for a number of years, to gather the texts together. The volume Mr. Davies edited for publication in England is made up solely of broadcasts as Dylan Thomas delivered them.

His American publisher, believing that American readers will prefer a broader and more complete collection of Thomas's stories and essays, has preferred to enlarge this edition of *Quite Early One Morning* to include a number of stories and articles published in magazines, and not broadcast. He has also preferred to print here the more finished versions of the broadcast talks, as Thomas revised them for publication.

Although the American edition of *Quite Early One Morning* differs considerably from the English edition, the publisher wishes to acknowledge his large debt to Mr. Davies for his great contribution to the preparation of this volume.

For permission to print here the commentary written by Dylan Thomas for the British Government film *Our Country,* grateful acknowledgement is made to the Controller of Her Britannic Majesty's Stationery Office. British Crown copyright reserved.

For permission to print stories which were first published in magazines, grateful acknowledgement is made to the editors of the following: *The Atlantic Monthly, Circus, Encounter, Harper's*

Bazaar, Harper's Magazine, The Listener, The London Magazine, New Verse, Time, Vogue, and *Wales.*

For permission to print the following poems, grateful acknowledgement is made to Jonathan Cape, Ltd., and Mrs. W. H. Davies ("The Inquest" and "The Bust" from *The Collected Poems* of W. H. Davies); J. M. Dent & Sons, Ltd. ("O what can you give me?" from *Gwalia Deserta* by Idris Davies); George Allen & Unwin, Ltd., and the Macmillan Co., New York ("Sacco Writes to His Son" from *Ha! Ha! Among the Trumpets,* and "Odi et Amo," "Christmas Holday," and "The Century" from *Raiders Dawn* by Alun Lewis); the executors of Wilfred Owen's estate ("Exposure," "Anthem for Doomed Youth," "Greater Love," "A Terre," and "Strange Meeting" by Wilfred Owen); the Fortune Press and Mr. Glyn Jones ("Esyllt" from *Poems* by Glyn Jones); and Faber and Faber, Ltd. ("The Child on the Cliffs" from *The Collected Poems* of Edward Thomas; and the title poem from *Angry Summer* by Idris Davies). The publisher wishes to thank Mrs. Idris Davies for permisson to publish the two poems by Idris Davies. Dylan Thomas's own poems are reprinted here by arrangement with the trustees of his estate.

PART ONE

REMINISCENCES OF CHILDHOOD

I like very much people telling me about their childhood, but they'll have to be quick or else I'll be telling them about mine.

I was born in a large Welsh town at the beginning of the Great War—an ugly, lovely town (or so it was and is to me), crawling, sprawling by a long and splendid curving shore where truant boys and sandfield boys and old men from nowhere, beach-combed, idled and paddled, watched the dock-bound ships or the ships steaming away into wonder and India, magic and China, countries bright with oranges and loud with lions; threw stones into the sea for the barking outcast dogs; made castles and forts and harbours and race tracks in the sand; and on Saturday summer afternoons listened to the brass band, watched the Punch and Judy, or hung about on the fringes of the crowd to hear the fierce religious speakers who shouted at the sea, as though it were wicked and wrong to roll in and out like that, white-horsed and full of fishes.

One man, I remember, used to take off his hat and set fire to his hair every now and then, but I do not remember what it proved, if it proved anything at all, except that he was a very interesting man.

This sea-town was my world; outside a strange Wales, coal-pitted, mountained, river-run, full, so far as I knew, of choirs and football teams and sheep and storybook tall hats and red flannel petticoats, moved about its business which was none of mine.

Beyond that unknown Wales with its wild names like peals of bells in the darkness, and its mountain men clothed in the skins of animals perhaps and always singing, lay England which was London and the country called the Front, from which many of our neighbours never came back. It was a country to which only young men travelled.

At the beginning, the only "front" I knew was the little lobby before our front door. I could not understand how so many people never returned from there, but later I grew to know more, though still without understanding, and carried a wooden rifle in the park and shot down the invisible unknown enemy like a flock of wild birds. And the park itself was a world within the world of the sea-town. Quite near where I lived, so near that on summer evenings I could listen in my bed to the voices of older children playing ball on the sloping paper-littered bank, the park was full of terrors and treasures. Though it was only a little park, it held within its borders of old tall trees, notched with our names and shabby from our climbing, as many secret places, caverns and forests, prairies and deserts, as a country somewhere at the end of the sea.

And though we would explore it one day, armed and desperate, from end to end, from the robbers' den to the pirates' cabin, the highwayman's inn to the cattle ranch, or the hidden room in the undergrowth, where we held beetle races, and lit the wood fires and roasted potatoes and talked about Africa, and the makes of motor cars, yet still the next day, it remained as unexplored as the Poles—a country just born and always changing.

There were many secret societies but you could belong only to one; and in blood or red ink, and a rusty pocketknife, with, of course, an instrument to remove stones from horses' feet, you signed your name at the foot of a terrible document, swore death to all the other societies, crossed your heart that you would divulge no secret and that if you did, you would consent to torture by slow fire, and undertook to carry out by yourself a feat of either daring or endurance. You could take your choice: would you climb to the top of the tallest and most dangerous tree, and from there hurl stones and insults at grown-up passers-by, especially postmen, or any other men in uniform? Or would you ring every doorbell in the terrace, not forgetting the doorbell of the man with the red face who kept dogs and ran fast? Or would you swim in the reservoir, which was forbidden and had angry swans, or would you eat a whole old jam jar full of mud?

There were many more alternatives. I chose one of endurance and for half an hour, it may have been longer or shorter, held up off the ground a very heavy broken pram we had found in a bush. I thought my back would break and the half hour felt like a day, but I preferred it to braving the red face and the dogs, or to swallowing tadpoles.

We knew every inhabitant of the park, every regular visitor, every nursemaid, every gardner, every old man. We knew the hour when the alarming retired policeman came in to look at the dahlias and the hour when the old lady arrived in the Bath chair with six Pekinese, and a pale girl to read aloud to her. I think she read the newspaper, but we always said she read the *Wizard*. The face of the old man who sat summer and winter on the bench looking over the reservoir, I can see clearly now and I wrote a poem long long after I'd left the park and the sea-town called:

THE HUNCHBACK IN THE PARK

The hunchback in the park
A solitary mister
Propped between trees and water
From the opening of the garden lock
That lets the trees and water enter
Until the Sunday sombre ball at dark

Eating bread from a newspaper
Drinking water from the chained cup
That the children filled with gravel
In the fountain basin where I sailed my ship
Slept at night in a dog kennel
But nobody chained him up.

Like the park birds he came early
Like the water he sat down
And Mister they called Hey mister
The truant boys from the town
Running when he had heard them clearly
On out of sound

Past lake and rockery
Laughing when he shook his paper
Hunchbacked in mockery
Through the loud zoo of the willow groves
Dodging the park-keeper
With his stick that picked up leaves.

And the old dog sleeper
Alone between nurses and swans
While the boys among willows
Made the tigers jump out of their eyes
To roar on the rockery stones
And the groves were blue with sailors

Made all day until bell-time
A woman figure without fault
Straight as a young elm
Straight and tall from his crooked bones
That she might stand in the night
After the locks and the chains

All night in the unmade park
After the railings and shrubberies
The birds the grass the trees and the lake
And the wild boys innocent as strawberries
Had followed the hunchback
To his kennel in the dark.

And that park grew up with me; that small world widened
as I learned its secrets and boundaries, as I discovered new refuges
and ambushes in its woods and jungles; hidden homes and lairs
for the multitudes of imagination, for cowboys and Indians, and
the tall terrible half-people who rode on nightmares through my
bedroom. But it was not the only world—that world of rockery,
gravel path, playbank, bowling green, bandstands, reservoir,
dahlia garden, where an ancient keeper, known as Smoky, was the
whiskered snake in the grass one must keep off. There was another world where with my friends I used to dawdle on half
holidays along the bent and Devon-facing seashore, hoping for
gold watches or the skull of a sheep or a message in a bottle to be
washed up with the tide; and another where we used to wander
whistling through the packed streets, stale as station sandwiches,
round the impressive gasworks and the slaughter house, past by
the blackened monuments and the museum that should have
been in a museum. Or we scratched at a kind of cricket on the
bald and cindery surface of the recreation ground, or we took a
tram that shook like an iron jelly down to the gaunt pier, there

to clamber under the pier, hanging perilously on to its skeleton legs or to run along to the end where the patient men with the seaward eyes of the dockside unemployed capped and mufflered, dangling from their mouths pipes that had long gone out, angled over the edge for unpleasant tasting fish.

Never was there such a town as ours, I thought, as we fought on the sandhills with rough boys or dared each other to climb up the scaffolding of half-built houses soon to be called Laburnum Beaches. Never was there such a town, I thought, for the smell of fish and chips on Saturday evenings; for the Saturday afternoon cinema matinees where we shouted and hissed our threepences away; for the crowds in the streets with leeks in their hats on international nights; for the park, the inexhaustible and mysterious, bushy red-Indian hiding park where the hunchback sat alone and the groves were blue with sailors. The memories of childhood have no order, and so I remember that never was there such a dame school as ours, so firm and kind and smelling of galoshes, with the sweet and fumbled music of the piano lessons drifting down from up-stairs to the lonely schoolroom, where only the sometimes tearful wicked sat over undone sums, or to repeat a little crime—the pull-ing of a girl's hair during geography, the sly shin kick under the table during English literature. Behind the school was a narrow lane where only the oldest and boldest threw pebbles at windows, scuffled and boasted, fibbed about their relations—

"My father's got a chauffeur."

"What's he want a chauffeur for? He hasn't got a car."

"My father's the richest man in the town."

"My father's the richest man in Wales."

"My father owns the world."

And swapped gob-stoppers for slings, old knives for marbles, kite strings for foreign stamps.

The lane was always the place to tell your secrets; if you did not have any, you invented them. Occasionally now I dream that I am turning out of school into the lane of confidences when I say to the boys of my class, "At last, I have a real secret."

"What is it—what is it?"

"I can fly."

And when they do not believe me, I flap my arms and slowly leave the ground only a few inches at first, then gaining air until I fly waving my cap level with the upper windows of the school, peering in until the mistress at the piano screams and the metronome falls to the ground and stops, and there is no more time.

And I fly over the trees and chimneys of my town, over the dockyards skimming the masts and funnels, over Inkerman Street, Sebastopol Street, and the street where all the women wear men's caps, over the trees of the everlasting park, where a brass band shakes the leaves and sends them showering down on to the nurses and the children, the cripples and the idlers, and the gardeners, and the shouting boys: over the yellow seashore, and the stone-chasing dogs, and the old men, and the singing sea.

The memories of childhood have no order, and no end.

(1943, 1953)

QUITE EARLY ONE MORNING

Quite early one morning in the winter in Wales, by the sea that was lying down still and green as grass after a night of tar-black howling and rolling, I went out of the house, where I had come to stay for a cold unseasonable holiday, to see if it was raining still, if the outhouse had been blown away, potatoes, shears, rat-killer, shrimpnets, and tins of rusty nails aloft on the wind, and if all the cliffs were left. It had been such a ferocious night that someone in the smoky ship-pictured bar had said he could feel his tombstone shaking even though he was not dead or, at least, was moving; but the morning shone as clear and calm as one always imagines tomorrow will shine.

The sun lit the sea-town, not as a whole—from topmost down —reproving zinc-roofed chapel to empty but for rats and whispers grey warehouse on the harbour, but in separate bright pieces. There, the quay shouldering out, nobody on it now but the gulls and the capstans like small men in tubular trousers. Here, the roof of the police station, black as a helmet, dry as a summons, sober as Sunday. There, the splashed church, with a cloud in the shape of a bell poised above it, ready to drift and ring. Here the chimneys of the pink-washed pub, the pub that was waiting for Saturday night as an overjolly girl waits for sailors.

The town was not yet awake. The milkman lay still, lost in the clangour and music of his Welsh-spoken dreams, the wish-fulfilled tenor voices, more powerful than Caruso's, sweeter than Ben Davies's, thrilling past Cloth Hall and Manchester House up to the frosty hills.

The town was not yet awake. Babies in upper bedrooms of salt-white houses dangling over water, or of bow-windowed villas squatting prim in neatly treed but unsteady hill-streets, worried the light with their half-in-sleep cries. Miscellaneous retired sea-captains emerged for a second from deeper waves than ever tossed their boats, then drowned again, going down, down into a perhaps Mediterranean-blue cabin of sleep, rocked to the sea-beat of their years. Landladies, shawled and bloused and aproned with sleep in the curtained, bombasined-black of their once spare rooms, remembered their loves, their bills, their visitors dead, decamped, or buried in English deserts till the trumpet of next expensive August roused them again to the world of holiday rain, dismal cliff and sand seen through the weeping windows of front parlours, tasselled tablecloths, stuffed pheasants, ferns in pots, fading photographs of the bearded and censorious dead, autograph albums with a look of limp and colourless beribboned hair, lolling out between the thick black boards.

The town was not yet awake. Birds sang in eaves, bushes, trees, on telegraph wires, rails, fences, spars and wet masts, not for love or joy, but to keep other birds away. The landlords in feathers disputed the right of even the flying light to descend and perch.

The town was not yet awake, and I walked through the streets like a stranger come out of the sea, shrugging off weed and wave and darkness with each step, or like an inquisitive shadow, determined to miss nothing: not the preliminary tremor in the throat of the dawn-saying cock or the first whirring nudge of arranged time in the belly of the alarm clock on the trinketed chest of drawers under the knitted text and the done-by-hand water colours of Porthcawl or Trinidad.

I walked past the small sea-spying windows, behind whose trim curtains lay mild-mannered men and women not yet awake and, for all I could know, terrible and violent in their dreams. In the head of Miss Hughes "The Cosy" clashed the cymbals of an Eastern court. Eunuchs struck gongs the size of Bethesda Chapel. Sultans with voices fiercer than visiting preachers demanded a most un-Welsh dance. Everywhere there glowed and rayed the colours of the small, slate-grey woman's dreams: purple, magenta, ruby, sapphire, emerald, vermilion, honey. But I could not believe it. She knitted in her tidy sleep-world a beige woollen shroud with "Thou Shalt Not" on the bosom.

I could not imagine Cadwallader Davies the grocer, in his near-to-waking dream, riding on horseback, two-gunned and Cody-bold, through the cactused prairies. He added, he subtracted, he receipted, he filed a prodigious account with a candle dipped in dried egg.

What big seas of dreams ran in the Captain's sleep? Over

what blue-whaled waves did he sail through a rainbow-hail of flying fishes to the music of Circe's swinish island? Do not let him be dreaming of dividends and bottled beer and onions.

Someone was snoring in one house. I counted ten savagely indignant grunts-and-groans like those of a pig in a model and mudless farm, which ended with a window-rattler, a washbasin-shaker, a trembler of tooth glasses, a waker of dormice. It thundered with me up to the chapel railings, then brassily vanished.

The chapel stood grim and grey, telling the day there was to be no nonsense. The chapel was not asleep; it never cat-napped nor nodded nor closed its long cold eye. I left it telling the morning off and a seagull hung, rebuked, above it.

And climbing down again, and up out of the town, I heard the cocks crow from hidden farmyards, from old roosts above waves, where fabulous seabirds might sit and cry, "Neptune!" And a faraway clock struck from another church, in another village, in another universe, though the wind blew the time away. And I walked in a timeless morning past a row of white cottages, almost expecting that an ancient man with a great beard and an hourglass and a scythe under his nightdressed arm might lean from a window and ask *me* the time. I would have told him: "Arise, old counter of the heartbeats of albatrosses, and wake the cavernous sleepers of the town to a dazzling new morning." I would have told him: "You unbelievable father of Eva and Dai Adam, come out, old chicken, and stir up the winter morning with your spoon of a scythe." I would have told him—I would have scampered like a scalding ghost, over the cliffs and down into the bilingual sea.

Who lived in those cottages? I was a stranger to the sea-town, fresh or stale from the city where I worked for my bread and butter, wishing it were laver-bread and country salty butter yoke-yellow. Fishermen, certainly; no painters but of boats, no man-dressed women with shooting-sticks and sketchbooks and voices like macaws, to paint the reluctant heads of critical and sturdy natives who posed by the pint, against the chapel-dark sea which would be made more blue than the Bay of Naples, though shallower.

I walked on to the cliff path again, the town behind and below waking up now so very slowly; I stopped, and turned, and looked. Smoke from one chimney. The cobbler's, I thought, but from that distance it may have been the chimney of the retired male-nurse who had come to live in Wales after many years' successful wrestling with the mad rich of southern England. He was not liked. He measured you for a strait jacket, carefully, with his eye. He saw you bounce from rubber walls like a sorbo ball. No behaviour surprised him. Many people of the town found it hard to resist leering at him suddenly around the corner, or convulsively dancing, or pointing with laughter and devilish good humour to invisible dogfights, merely to prove to him that they were "normal."

Smoke from another chimney now: they were burning their last night's dreams: up from a chimney came a long-haired wraith, like an old politician: somebody had been dreaming of the Liberal party. But no, the smoky figure wove, attenuated into a refined and precise grey comma: someone had been dreaming of reading Charles Morgan.

Oh! the town was waking now and I heard distinctly, insistent over the slow-speaking sea, the voices of the town blown up to me. And some of the voices said:

I am Miss May Hughes "The Cosy," a lonely lady,
    waiting in her house by the nasty sea,
waiting for her husband and pretty baby
    to come home at last from wherever they may be.

I am Captain Tiny Evans, my ship was the *Kidwelly*,
    and Mrs. Tiny Evans has been dead for many a year.
Poor Captain Tiny all alone, the neighbours whisper,
    but I liked it all alone and I hated her.

Clara Tawe Jenkins, "Madame" they call me,
    an old contralto with her dressing gown on.
And I sit at the window and I sing to the sea,
    for the sea doesn't notice that my voice has gone.

Parchedig Thomas Evans making morning tea,
    very weak tea, too, you mustn't waste a leaf.
Every morning making tea in my house by the sea,
    I am troubled by one thing only, and that's—Belief.

Open the curtains, light the fire, what are servants for?
    I am Mrs. Ogmore-Pritchard and I want another snooze.
Dust the china, feed the canary, sweep the drawing-room floor.
    And before you let the sun in, mind he wipes his shoes.

I am only Mr. Griffiths, very shortsighted, B.A., Aber.
    As soon as I finish my egg I must shuffle off to school.
Oh, patron saint of teachers, teach me to keep order,
    and *forget* those words on the blackboard—"Griffiths Bat is
        a fool."

Do you hear that whistling?—It's me, I am Phoebe,
    the maid at the King's Head, and I am whistling like a bird.
Someone split a tin of pepper in the tea.
    There's twenty for breakfast, and I'm not going to say a word.

    Thus some of the voices of a cliff-perched town at the far end
of Wales moved out of sleep and darkness into the newborn,
ancient and ageless morning, moved and were lost.

                                                        (*1945*)

A CHILD'S CHRISTMAS IN WALES

One Christmas was so much like another, in those years around the sea-town corner now and out of all sound except the distant speaking of the voices I sometimes hear a moment before sleep, that I can never remember whether it snowed for six days and six nights when I was twelve or whether it snowed for twelve days and twelve nights when I was six. All the Christmases roll down toward the two-tongued sea, like a cold and headlong moon bundling down the sky that was our street; and they stop at the rim of the ice-edged, fish-freezing waves, and I plunge my hands in the snow and bring out whatever I can find. In goes my hand into that wool-white bell-tongued ball of holidays resting at the rim of the carol-singing sea, and out come Mrs. Prothero and the firemen.

It was on the afternoon of the day of Christmas Eve, and I was in Mrs. Prothero's garden, waiting for cats, with her son Jim. It was snowing. It was always snowing at Christmas. December, in my memory, is white as Lapland, though there were no reindeers. But there were cats. Patient, cold and callous, our hands wrapped in socks, we waited to snowball the cats. Sleek and long as jaguars and horrible-whiskered, spitting and snarling, they would slink and sidle over the white back-garden walls, and the lynx-eyed hunters, Jim and I, fur-capped and moccasined trappers from Hudson Bay, off Mumbles Road, would hurl our deadly snowballs at the green of their eyes. The wise cats never appeared. We were so still, Eskimo-footed arctic marksmen in the muffling silence of the eternal snows—eternal, ever since Wednesday—that we never heard Mrs. Prothero's first cry from her igloo at the bottom of the garden. Or, if we heard it at all, it was, to us, like the far-off challenge of our enemy and prey, the neighbour's polar cat. But soon the voice grew louder.

"Fire!" cried Mrs. Prothero, and she beat the dinner-gong.

And we ran down the garden, with the snowballs in our arms, toward the house; and smoke, indeed, was pouring out of the dining-room, and the bong was bombilating, and Mrs. Prothero was announcing ruin like a town crier in Pompeii. This was better than all the cats in Wales standing on the wall in a row. We bounded into the house, laden with snowballs, and stopped at the open door of the smoke-filled room. Something was burning all right; perhaps it was Mr. Prothero, who always slept there after midday dinner with a newspaper over his face. But he was standing in the middle of the room, saying, "A fine Christmas!" and smacking at the smoke with a slipper.

"Call the fire brigade," cried Mrs. Prothero as she beat the gong.

"They won't be there," said Mr. Prothero, "it's Christmas."

There was no fire to be seen, only clouds of smoke and Mr. Prothero standing in the middle of them, waving his slipper as though he were conducting.

"Do something," he said.

And we threw all our snowballs into the smoke—I think we missed Mr. Prothero—and ran out of the house to the telephone box.

"Let's call the police as well," Jim said.

"And the ambulance."

"And Ernie Jenkins, he likes fires."

But we only called the fire brigade, and soon the fire engine came and three tall men in helmets brought a hose into the house and Mr. Prothero got out just in time before they turned it on. Nobody could have had a noiser Christmas Eve. And when the fireman turned off the hose and were standing in the wet, smoky room, Jim's aunt, Miss Prothero, came downstairs and peered in at them. Jim and I waited, very quietly, to hear what she would say to them. She said the right thing, always. She looked at the three tall firemen in their shining helmets, standing among the smoke and cinders and dissolving snowballs, and she said: "Would you like anything to read?"

Years and years and years ago, when I was a boy, when there were wolves in Wales, and birds the color of red-flannel petticoats whisked past the harp-shaped hills, when we sang and wallowed all night and day in caves that smelt like Sunday afternoons in damp front farmhouses parlors, and we chased, with the jawbones of deacons, the English and the bears, before the motor car, before the wheel, before the duchess-faced horse when we rode the daft and happy hills bareback, it snowed and it snowed. But here a small boy says: "It snowed last year, too. I made a snowman and my brother knocked it down and I knocked my brother down and then we had tea."

"But that was not the same snow," I say. "Our snow was not only shaken from whitewash buckets down the sky, it came shawling out of the ground and swam and drifted out of the arms and hands and bodies of the trees; snow grew overnight on the roofs of the houses like a pure and grandfather moss, minutely white-ivied the walls and settled on the postman, opening the gate, like a dumb, numb thunderstorm of white, torn Christmas cards."

"Were there postmen then, too?"

"With sprinkling eyes and wind-cherried noses, on spread, frozen feet they crunched up to the doors and mittened on them manfully. But all that the children could hear was a ringing of bells."

"You mean that the postman went rat-a-tat-tat and the doors rang?"

"I mean that the bells that the children could hear were inside them."

"I only hear thunder sometimes, never bells."

"There were church bells, too."

"Inside them?"

"No, no, no, in the bat-black, snow-white belfries, tugged by bishops and storks. And they rang their tidings over the bandaged town, over the frozen foam of the powder and ice-cream hills, over the crackling sea. It seemed that all the churches boomed for joy under my window; and the weathercocks crew for Christmas, on our fence."

"Get back to the postmen."

"They were just ordinary postmen, fond of walking and dogs and Christmas and the snow. They knocked on the doors with blue knuckles. . . ."

"Ours has got a black knocker. . . ."

"And then they stood on the white Welcome mat in the little, drifted porches and huffed and puffed, making ghosts with their breath, and jogged from foot to foot like small boys wanting to go out."

"And then the Presents?"

"And then the Presents, after the Christmas box. And the

cold postman, with a rose on his button-nose, tingled down the tea-tray-slithered run of the chilly glinting hill. He went in his ice-bound boots like a man on fishmonger's slabs. He wagged his bag like a frozen camel's hump, dizzily turned the corner on one foot, and, by God, he was gone."

"Get back to the Presents."

"There were the Useful Presents: engulfing mufflers of the old coach days, and mittens made for giant sloths; zebra scarfs of a substance like silky gum that could be tug-o'-warred down to the galoshes; blinding tam-o'-shanters like patchwork tea cozies and bunny-suited busbies and balaclavas for victims of head-shrinking tribes; from aunts who always wore wool next to the skin there were mustached and rasping vests that made you wonder why the aunts had any skin left at all; and once I had a little crocheted nose bag from an aunt now, alas, no longer whinnying with us. And pictureless books in which small boys, though warned with quotations not to, *would* skate on Farmer Giles' pond and did and drowned; and books that told me everything about the wasp, except why."

"Go on to the Useless Presents."

"Bags of moist and many-colored jelly babies and a folded flag and a false nose and a tram-conductor's cap and a machine that punched tickets and rang a bell; never a catapult; once, by mistake that no one could explain, a little hatchet; and a celluloid duck that made, when you pressed it, a most unducklike sound, a mewing moo that an ambitious cat might make who wished to be a cow; and a painting book in which I could make the grass, the trees, the sea and the animals any color I pleased, and still the dazzling sky-blue sheep are grazing in the red field under the rainbow-billed and pea-green birds. Hard-boileds, toffee, fudge and allsorts, crunches, cracknels, humbugs, glaciers, marzipan, and butterwelsh for the Welsh. And troops of bright tin soldiers who, if they could not fight, could always run. And Snakes-and-Families and Happy Ladders. And Easy Hobbi-Games for Little Engineers, complete with instructions. Oh, easy for Leonardo! And a whistle to make the dogs bark to wake up the old man next door to make him beat on the wall with his stick to shake our picture off the wall. And a packet of cigarettes: you put one in your mouth and you stood at the corner of the street and you waited for hours, in vain, for an old lady to scold you for smoking a cigarette, and then with a smirk you ate it. And then it was breakfast under the balloons."

"Were there Uncles, like in our house?"

"There are always Uncles at Christmas. The same Uncles. And on Christmas mornings, with dog-disturbing whistle and sugar fags, I would scour the swatched town for the news of the little world, and find always a dead bird by the white Post Office or by the deserted swings; perhaps a robin, all but one of his fires out. Men and women wading or scooping back from chapel, with taproom noses and wind-bussed cheeks, all albinos, huddled their stiff black jarring feathers against the irreligious snow. Mistletoe hung from the gas brackets in all the front parlors; there was sherry and walnuts and bottled beer and crackers by the dessertspoons; and cats in their fur-abouts watched the fires; and the high-heaped fire spat, all ready for the chestnuts and the mulling pokers. Some few large men sat in the front parlors, without their collars, Uncles almost certainly, trying their new cigars, holding them out judiciously at arms' length, returning them to their mouths, coughing, then holding them out again as though waiting for the explosion; and some few small aunts, not wanted in the kitchen, nor anywhere else for that matter, sat on the very edges of their chairs, poised and brittle, afraid to break, like faded cups and saucers."

Not many those mornings trod the piling streets: an old man always, fawn-bowlered, yellow-gloved and, at this time of year, with spats of snow, would take his constitutional to the white bowling green and back, as he would take it wet or fine on Christmas Day or Doomsday; sometimes two hale young men, with big pipes blazing, no overcoats and wind-blown scarfs, would trudge, unspeaking, down to the forlorn sea, to work up an appetite, to blow away the fumes, who knows, to walk into the waves until nothing of them was left but the two curling smoke clouds of their inextinguishable briars. Then I would be slapdashing home, the gravy smell of the dinners of others, the bird smell, the brandy, the pudding and mince, coiling up to my nostrils, when out of a snow-clogged side lane would come a boy the spit of myself, with a pink-tipped cigarette and the violet past of a black eye, cocky as a bullfinch, leering all to himself. I hated him on sight and sound, and would be about to put my dog whistle to my lips and blow him off the face of Christmas when suddenly he, with a violet wink, put *his* whistle to *his* lips and blew so stridently, so high, so exquisitely loud, that gobbling faces, their cheeks bulged with goose, would press against their tinseled windows, the whole length of the white echoing street. For dinner we had turkey and blazing pudding, and after dinner the Uncles sat in front of the fire, loosened all buttons, put their large moist hands over their watch chains, groaned a little and slept. Mothers, aunts and sisters scuttled to and fro, bearing tureens. Auntie Bessie, who had already been frightened, twice, by a clock-work mouse, whimpered at the sideboard and had some elderberry wine. The dog was sick. Auntie Dosie had to have three aspirins, but Auntie Hannah, who liked port, stood in the middle of the snowbound back yard, singing like a big-bosomed thrush. I would blow up balloons to see how big they would blow up to; and, when they burst, which they all did, the Uncles jumped and rumbled. In the rich and heavy afternoon, the Uncles breathing like dolphins and the snow descending, I would sit among festoons and Chinese lanterns and nibble dates and try to make a model man-o'-war, following the Instructions for Little Engineers, and produce what might be mistaken for a sea-going tramcar. Or I would go out, my bright new boots squeaking, into the white world, on to the seaward hill, to call on Jim and Dan and Jack and to pad through the still streets, leaving huge deep footprints on the hidden pavements.

"I bet people will think there's been hippos."

"What would you do if you saw a hippo coming down our street?"

"I'd go like this, bang! I'd throw him over the railings and roll him down the hill and then I'd tickle him under the ear and he'd wag his tail."

"What would you do if you saw *two* hippos?"

Iron-flanked and bellowing he-hippos clanked and battered through the scudding snow toward us as we passed Mr. Daniel's house.

"Let's post Mr. Daniel a snowball through his letter box."

"Let's write things in the snow."

"Let's write, 'Mr. Daniel looks like a spaniel' all over his lawn."

Or we walked on the white shore. "Can the fishes see it's snowing?"

The silent one-clouded heavens drifted on to the sea. Now we were snow-blind travelers lost on the north hills, and vast dewlapped dogs, with flasks round their necks, ambled and shambled up to us, baying "Excelsior." We returned home through the poor streets where only a few children fumbled with bare red fingers in the wheel-rutted snow and catcalled after us, their voices fading away, as we trudged uphill, into the cries of the dock birds and the hooting of ships out in the whirling bay. And then, at tea the recovered Uncles would be jolly; and the ice cake loomed in the center of the table like a marble grave. Auntie Hannah laced her tea with rum, because it was only once a year.

Bring out the tall tales now that we told by the fire as the gaslight bubbled like a diver. Ghosts whooed like owls in the long nights when I dared not look over my shoulder; animals lurked in the cubbyhole under the stairs where the gas meter ticked. And I remember that we went singing carols once, when there wasn't the shaving of a moon to light the flying street. At the end of a long road was a drive that led to a large house, and we stumbled up the darkness of the drive that night, each one of us afraid, each one holding a stone in his hand in case, and all of us too brave to say a word. The wind through the trees made noises as of old and unpleasant and maybe webfooted men wheezing in caves. We reached the black bulk of the house.

"What shall we give them? Hark the Herald?"

"No," Jack said, "Good King Wenceslas. I'll count three."

One, two, three, and we began to sing, our voices high and seemingly distant in the snow-felted darkness round the house that was occupied by nobody we knew. We stood close together, near the dark door.

> Good King Wenceslas looked out
> On the Feast of Stephen . . .

And then a small, dry voice, like the voice of someone who has not spoken for a long time, joined our singing: a small, dry, eggshell voice from the other side of the door: a small dry voice through the keyhole. And when we stopped running we were outside *our* house; the front room was lovely; balloons floated under the hot-water-bottle-gulping gas; everything was good again and shone over the town.

"Perhaps it was a ghost," Jim said.

"Perhaps it was trolls," Dan said, who was always reading.

"Let's go in and see if there's any jelly left," Jack said. And we did that.

Always on Christmas night there was music. An uncle played the fiddle, a cousin sang "Cherry Ripe," and another uncle sang "Drake's Drum." It was very warm in the little house. Auntie Hannah, who had got on to the parsnip wine, sang about Bleeding Hearts and Death, and then another in which she said her heart was like a Bird's Nest; and then everybody laughed again; and then I went to bed. Looking through my bedroom window, out into the moonlight and the unending smoke-colored snow, I could see the lights in the windows of all the other houses on our hill and hear the music rising from them up the long, steadily falling night. I turned the gas down, I got into bed. I said some words to the close and holy darkness, and then I slept.

(1945, 1950)

HOLIDAY MEMORY

August Bank Holiday—a tune on an ice-cream cornet. A slap of sea and a tickle of sand. A fanfare of sunshades opening. A wince and whinny of bathers dancing into deceptive water. A tuck of dresses. A rolling of trousers. A compromise of paddlers. A sunburn of girls and a lark of boys. A silent hullabaloo of balloons.

I remember the sea telling lies in a shell held to my ear for a whole harmonious, hollow minute by a small, wet girl in an enormous bathing suit marked Corporation Property.

I remember sharing the last of my moist buns with a boy and a lion. Tawny and savage, with cruel nails and capacious mouth, the little boy tore and devoured. Wild as seedcake, ferocious as a hearthrug, the depressed and verminous lion nibbled like a mouse at his half a bun and hiccupped in the sad dusk of his cage.

I remember a man like an alderman or a bailiff, bowlered and collarless, with a bag of monkeynuts in his hand, crying "Ride 'em, cowboy!" time and again as he whirled in his chairaplane giddily above the upturned laughing faces of the town girls bold as brass and the boys with padded shoulders and shoes sharp as knives; and the monkeynuts flew through the air like salty hail.

Children all day capered or squealed by the glazed or bashing sea, and the steam-organ wheezed its waltzes in the threadbare playground and the waste lot, where the dodgems dodged, behind the pickle factory.

And mothers loudly warned their proud pink daughters or sons to put that jellyfish down; and fathers spread newspapers over their faces; and sandfleas hopped on the picnic lettuce; and someone had forgotten the salt.

In those always radiant, rainless, lazily rowdy and skyblue summers departed, I remember August Monday from the rising of the sun over the stained and royal town to the husky hushing of the roundabout music and the dowsing of the naphtha jets in the seaside fair: from bubble-and-squeak to the last of the sandy sandwiches.

There was no need, that holiday morning, for the sluggardly

boys to be shouted down to breakfast; out of their jumbled beds they tumbled, and scrambled into rumpled clothes; quickly at the bathroom basin they catlicked their hands and faces, but never forgot to run the water loud and long as though they washed like colliers; in front of the cracked looking-glass, bordered with cigarette cards, in their treasure-trove bedrooms, they whisked a gap-tooth comb through their surly hair; and with shining cheeks and noses and tidemarked necks, they took the stairs three at a time.

But for all their scramble and scamper, clamour on the landing, catlick and toothbrush flick, hair-whisk and stair-jump, their sisters were always there before them. Up with the lady lark, they had prinked and frizzed and hot-ironed; and smug in their blossoming dresses, ribboned for the sun, in gymshoes white as the blanco'd snow, neat and silly with doilies and tomatoes they helped in the higgledy kitchen. They were calm; they were virtuous; they had washed their necks; they did not romp, or fidget; and only the smallest sister put out her tongue at the noisy boys.

And the woman who lived next door came into the kitchen and said that her mother, an ancient uncertain body who wore a hat with cherries, was having one of her days and had insisted, that very holiday morning, in carrying, all the way to the tram-stop, a photograph album and the cutglass fruit bowl from the front room.

This was the morning when father, mending one hole in the thermos-flask, made three; when the sun declared war on the butter, and the butter ran; when dogs, with all the sweet-binned backyards to wag and sniff and bicker in, chased their tails in the jostling kitchen, worried sandshoes, snapped at flies, writhed between legs, scratched among towels, sat smiling on hampers.

And if you could have listened at some of the open doors of some of the houses in the street you might have heard:—

"Uncle Owen says he can't find the bottle-opener—"
  "Has he looked under the hallstand?"
"Willy's cut his finger—"
  "Got your spade?"
"If somebody doesn't kill that dog—"
"Uncle Owen says why should the bottle-opener be under the hallstand?"
  "Never again, never again—"

"I know I put the pepper somewhere—"
     "Willy's bleeding—"
"Look, there's a bootlace in my bucket—"
     "Oh come *on*, come *on*—"
"Let's have a look at the bootlace in your bucket—"
     "If I lay my hands on that dog—"
"Uncle Owen's found the bottle-opener—"
     "Willy's bleeding over the cheese—"

And the trams that hissed like ganders took us all to the beautiful beach.

There was cricket on the sand, and sand in the spongecake, sandflies in the watercress, and foolish, mulish, religious donkeys on the unwilling trot. Girls undressed in slipping tents of propriety; under invisible umbrellas, stout ladies dressed for the male and immoral sea. Little naked navvies dug canals; children with spades and no ambition built fleeting castles; wispy young men, outside the bathing-huts, whistled at substantial young women and dogs who desired thrown stones more than the bones of elephants. Recalcitrant uncles huddled, over luke ale, in the tiger-striped marquees. Mothers in black, like wobbling mountains, gasped under the discarded dresses of daughters who shrilly braved the gobbling waves. And fathers, in the once-a-year sun, took fifty winks. Oh, think of all the fifty winks along the paper-bagged sand.

Liquorice allsorts, and Welsh hearts, were melting. And the sticks of rock, that we all sucked, were like barbers' poles made of rhubarb.

In the distance, surrounded by disappointed theoreticians and an ironmonger with a drum, a cross man on an orange-box shouted that holidays were wrong. And the waves rolled in, with rubber ducks and clerks upon them.

I remember the patient, laborious, and enamouring hobby, or profession, of burying relatives in sand.

I remember the princely pastime of pouring sand, from cupped hands or bucket, down collars of tops of dresses; the shriek, the shake, the slap.

I can remember the boy by himself, the beachcombing lone-wolf, hungrily waiting at the edge of family cricket; the friendless fielder, the boy uninvited to bat or to tea.

I remember the smell of sea and seaweed, wet flesh, wet hair, wet bathing-dresses, the warm smell as of a rabbity field after rain, the smell of pop and splashed sunshades and toffee, the stable-and-straw smell of hot, tossed, tumbled, dug and trodden sand, the swill-and-gaslamp smell of Saturday night, though the sun shone strong, from the bellying beer-tents, the smell of the vinegar on shelled cockles, winkle-smell, shrimp-smell, the dripping-oily back-street winter-smell of chips in newspapers, the smell of ships from the sundazed docks round the corner of the sandhills, the smell of the known and paddled-in sea moving, full of the drowned and herrings, out and away and beyond and further still towards the antipodes that hung their koala-bears and Maoris, kangaroos and boomerangs, upside down over the back of the stars.

And the noise of pummelling Punch and Judy falling, and a clock tolling or telling no time in the tenantless town; now and again a bell from a lost tower or a train on the lines behind us clearing its throat, and always the hopeless, ravenous swearing and pleading of the gulls, donkey-bray and hawker-cry, harmonicas and toy trumpets, shouting and laughing and singing, hooting of tugs and tramps, the clip of the chair-attendant's puncher, the motorboat coughing in the bay, and the same hymn and washing of the sea that was heard in the Bible.

"If it could only just, if it could only just," your lips said again and again as you scooped, in the hob-hot sand, dungeons, garages, torture-chambers, train tunnels, arsenals, hangars for zeppelins, witches' kitchens, vampires' parlours, smugglers' cellars, trolls' grog-shops, sewers, under the ponderous and cracking castle, "If it could only just be like this for ever and ever amen." August Monday all over the earth, from Mumbles where the aunties grew like ladies on a seaside tree to brown, bear-hugging Henty-land and the turtled Ballantyne Islands.

"Could donkeys go on the ice?"
"Only if they got snowshoes."

We snowshoed a meek, complaining donkey and galloped him off in the wake of the ten-foot-tall and Atlas-muscled Mounties, rifled and pemmicanned, who always, in the white Gold Rush wastes, got their black-oathed-and-bearded Man.

"Are there donkeys on desert islands?"

"Only sort-of-donkeys."

"What d'you mean, sort-of donkeys?"

"Native donkeys. They hunt things on them!"

"Sort-of walruses and seals and things?"

"Donkeys can't swim!"

"These donkeys can. They swim like whales, they swim like anything, they swim like—"

"Liar."

"Liar yourself."

And two small boys fought fiercely and silently in the sand, rolling together in a ball of legs and bottoms. Then they went and saw the pierrots, or bought vanilla ices.

Lolling or larriking that unsoiled, boiling beauty of a common day, great gods with their braces over their vests sang, spat pips, puffed smoke at wasps, gulped and ogled, forgot the rent, embraced, posed for the dicky-bird, were coarse, had rainbow-coloured armpits, winked, belched, blamed the radishes, looked at Ilfracombe, played hymns on paper and comb, peeled bananas, scratched, found seaweed in their panamas, blew up paper-bags and banged them, wished for nothing. But over all the beautiful beach I remember most the children playing, boys and girls tumbling, moving jewels, who might never be happy again. And "happy as a sandboy" is true as the heat of the sun.

Dusk came down; or grew up out of the sands and the sea; or curled around us from the calling docks and the bloodily smoking sun. The day was done, the sands brushed and ruffled suddenly with a sea-broom of cold wind. And we gathered together all the spades and buckets and towels, empty hampers and bottles, umbrellas and fishfrails, bats and balls and knitting, and went—oh, listen, Dad!—to the Fair in the dusk on the bald seaside field.

Fairs were no good in the day; then they were shoddy and tired; the voices of hoopla girls were crimped as elocutionists; no cannonball could shake the roosting coconuts; the gondolas mechanically repeated their sober lurch; the Wall of Death was safe as a governess-cart; the wooden animals were waiting for the night.

But in the night, the hoopla girls, like operatic crows,

croaked at the coming moon; whizz, whirl, and ten for a tanner, the coconuts rained from their sawdust like grouse from the Highland sky; tipsy the griffon-prowed gondolas weaved on dizzy rails, and the Wall of Death was a spinning rim of ruin, and the neighing wooden horses took, to a haunting hunting tune, a thousand Beecher's Brooks as easily and breezily as hooved swallows.

Approaching, at dusk, the Fair-field from the beach, we scorched and gritty boys heard above the belabouring of the batherless sea the siren voices of the raucous, horsy barkers.

"Roll up, roll up!"

In her tent and her rolls of flesh the Fattest Woman in the World sat sewing her winter frock, another tent, and fixed her little eyes, blackcurrants in blancmange, on the skeletons who filed and sniggered by.

"Roll up, roll up, roll up to see the Largest Rat on the Earth, the Rover or Bonzo of vermin."

Here scampered the smallest pony, like a Shetland shrew, And here the Most Intelligent Fleas, trained, reined, bridled, and bitted, minutely cavorted in their glass corral.

Round galleries and shies and stalls, pennies were burning holes in a hundred pockets. Pale young men with larded hair and Valentino-black sidewhiskers, fags stuck to their lower lips, squinted along their swivel-sighted rifles and aimed at ping-pong balls dancing on fountains. In knife-creased, silver-grey, skirt-like Oxford bags, and a sleeveless, scarlet, zip-fastened shirt with yellow horizontal stripes, a collier at the strength-machine spat on his hands, raised the hammer, and brought it Thor-ing down. The bell rang for Blaina.

Outside his booth stood a bitten-eared and barn-door-chested pug with a nose like a twisted swede and hair that startled from his eyebrows and three teeth yellow as a camel's, inviting any sportsman to a sudden and sickening basting in the sandy ring or a quid if he lasted a round; and wiry, cocky, bowlegged, coal-scarred, boozed sportsmen by the dozen strutted in and reeled out; and still those three teeth remained, chipped and camel-yellow in the bored, teak face.

Draggled and stout-wanting mothers, with haphazard hats, hostile hatpins, buns awry, bursting bags, and children at their skirts like pop-filled and jam-smeared limpets, screamed, before distorting mirrors, at their suddenly tapering or tubular bodies and huge ballooning heads, and the children gaily bellowed at their own reflected bogies withering and bulging in the glass.

Old men, smelling of Milford Haven in the rain, shuffled, badgering and cadging, round the edges of the swaggering crowd, their only wares a handful of damp confetti. A daring dash of schoolboys, safely, shoulder to shoulder, with their fathers' trilbies cocked at a desperate angle over one eye, winked at and whistled after the procession past the swings of two girls arm-in-arm: always one pert and pretty, and always one with glasses. Girls in skulled and crossboned tunnels shrieked, and were comforted. Young men, heroic after pints, stood up on the flying chairaplanes, tousled, crimson, and against the rules. Jaunty girls gave sailors sauce.

All the Fun of the Fair in the hot, bubbling night. The Man in the sand-yellow Moon over the hurdy of gurdies. The swing-boats swimming to and fro like slices of the moon. Dragons and hippogriffs at the prows of the gondolas breathing fire and Sousa. Midnight roundabout riders tantivying under the fairylights, huntsmen on billygoats and zebras hallooing under a circle of glow-worms.

And as we climbed home, up the gas-lit hill, to the still house over the mumbling bay, we heard the music die and the voices drift like sand. And we saw the lights of the Fair fade. And, at the far end of seaside field, they lit their lamps, one by one, in the caravans.

(1946)

If you can call it a story. There's no real beginning or end and there's very little in the middle. It is all about a day's outing, by charabanc, to Porthcawl, which, of course, the charabanc never reached, and it happened when I was so high and much nicer.

I was staying at the time with my uncle and his wife. Although she was my aunt, I never thought of her as anything but the wife of my uncle, partly because he was so big and trumpeting and red-hairy and used to fill every inch of the hot little house like an old buffalo squeezed into an airing cupboard, and partly because she was so small and silk and quick and made no noise at all as she whisked about on padded paws, dusting the china dogs, feeding the buffalo, setting the mousetraps that never caught her; and once she sleaked out of the room, to squeak in a nook or nibble in the hayloft, you forgot she had ever been there.

But there he was, always, a steaming hulk of an uncle, his braces straining like hawsers, crammed behind the counter of the tiny shop at the front of the house, and breathing like a brass band; or guzzling and blustery in the kitchen over his gutsy supper, too big for everything except the great black boats of his boots. As he ate, the house grew smaller; he billowed out over the furniture, the loud check meadow of his waistcoat littered, as though after a picnic, with cigarette ends, peelings, cabbage stalks, birds' bones, gravy; and the forest fire of his hair crackled among the hooked hams from the ceiling. She was so small she could hit him only if she stood on a chair; and every Saturday night at half-past ten he would lift her up, under his arm, onto a chair in the kitchen so that she could hit him on the head with whatever was handy, which was always a china dog. On Sundays, and when pickled, he sang high tenor, and had won many cups.

The first I heard of the annual outing was when I was sitting one evening on a bag of rice behind the counter, under one of my uncle's stomachs, reading an advertisement for sheep-dip, which was all there was to read. The shop was full of my uncle, and when Mr. Benjamin Franklyn, Mr. Weazley, Noah Bowen, and Will Sentry came in, I thought it would burst. It was like all being together in a drawer that smelled of cheese and turps, and twist tobacco and sweet biscuits and snuff and waistcoat. Mr. Benjamin Franklyn said that he had collected enough money for the charabanc and twenty cases of pale ale and a pound apiece over that he would distribute among the members of the outing when they first stopped for refreshment, and he was about sick and tired, he said, of being followed by Will Sentry.

"All day long, wherever I go," he said, "he's after me like a collie with one eye. I got a shadow of my own *and* a dog. I don't need no Tom, Dick or Harry pursuing me with his dirty muffler on."

Will Sentry blushed, and said, "It's only oily. I got a bicycle."

"A man has no privacy at all," Mr. Franklyn went on. "I tell you he sticks so close I'm afraid to go out the back in case I sit in his lap. It's a wonder to me," he said, "he don't follow me into bed at night."

"Wife won't let," Will Sentry said.

And that started Mr. Franklyn off again, and they tried to soothe him down by saying, "Don't you mind Will Sentry." "No harm in old Will." "He's only keeping an eye on the money, Benjie."

"Aren't I honest?" asked Mr. Franklyn in surprise. There was no answer for some time; then Noah Bowen said, "You know what the committee is. Ever since Bob the Fiddle they don't feel safe with a new treasurer."

"Do you think *I'm* going to drink the outing funds, like Bob the Fiddle did?" said Mr. Franklyn.

"You *might*," said my uncle, slowly.

"I resign," said Mr. Franklyn.

"Not with our money you won't," Will Sentry said.

"Who put the dynamite in the salmon pool?" said Mr. Weazley, but nobody took any notice of him. And, after a time, they all began to play cards in the thickening dusk of the hot, cheesy shop, and my uncle blew and bugled whenever he won, and Mr. Weazley grumbled like a dredger, and I fell to sleep on the gravy-scented mountain meadow of uncle's waistcoat.

On Sunday evening, after Bethesda, Mr. Franklyn walked into the kitchen where my uncle and I were eating sardines from the tin with spoons because it was Sunday and his wife would not let us play draughts. She was somewhere in the kitchen, too. Perhaps she was inside the grandmother clock, hanging from the weights and breathing. Then, a second later, the door opened again and Will Sentry edged into the room, twiddling his hard, round hat. He and Mr. Franklyn sat down on the settee, stiff and moth-balled and black in their chapel and funeral suits.

"I brought the list," said Mr. Franklyn. "Every member fully paid. You ask Will Sentry."

My uncle put on his spectacles, wiped his whiskery mouth with a handkerchief big as a Union Jack, laid down his spoon of sardines, took Mr. Franklyn's list of names, removed the spectacles so that he could read, and then ticked the names off one by one.

"Enoch Davies. Aye. He's good with his fists. You never know. Little Gerwain. Very melodious bass. Mr. Cadwalladwr. That's right. He can tell opening time better than my watch. Mr. Weazley. Of course. He's been to Paris. Pity he suffers so much in the charabanc. Stopped us nine times last year between the Beehive and the Red Dragon. Noah Bowen. Ah, very peaceable. He's got a tongue like a turtledove. Never a argument with Noah Bowen. Jenkins Loughor. Keep him off economics. It cost us a plate-glass window. And ten pints for the Sergeant. Mr. Jervis. Very tidy."

"He tried to put a pig in the charra," Will Sentry said.

"Live and let live," said my uncle.

Will Sentry blushed.

"Sinbad the Sailor's Arms. Got to keep in with him. Old O. Jones."

"Why old O. Jones?" said Will Sentry.

"Old O. Jones always goes," said my uncle.

I looked down at the kitchen table. The tin of sardines was gone. By Gee, I said to myself, Uncle's wife is quick as a flash.

"Cuthbert Johnny Fortnight. Now there's a card," said my uncle.

"He whistles after women," Will Sentry said.

"So do you," said Mr. Benjamin Franklyn, "in your mind."

My uncle at last approved the whole list, pausing only to say, when he came across one name, "If we weren't a Christian community, we'd chuck that Bob the Fiddle in the sea."

"We can do that in Porthcawl," said Mr. Franklyn, and soon

after that he went, Will Sentry no more than an inch behind him, their Sunday-bright boots squeaking on the kitchen cobbles.

And then, suddenly, there was my uncle's wife standing in front of the dresser, with a china dog in one hand. By Gee, I said to myself again, did you ever see such a woman, if that's what she is. The lamps were not lit yet in the kitchen and she stood in a wood of shadows, with the plates on the dresser behind her shining—like pink-and-white eyes.

"If you go on that outing on Saturday, Mr. Thomas," she said to my uncle in her small, silk voice, "I'm going home to my mother's."

Holy Mo, I thought, she's got a mother. Now that's one old bald mouse of a hundred and five I won't be wanting to meet in a dark lane.

"It's me or the outing, Mr. Thomas."

I would have made my choice at once, but it was almost half a minute before my uncle said, "Well, then, Sarah, it's the outing, my love." He lifted her up, under his arm, onto a chair in the kitchen, and she hit him on the head with the china dog. Then he lifted her down again, and then I said good night.

For the rest of the week my uncle's wife whisked quiet and quick round the house with her darting duster, my uncle blew and bugled and swole, and I kept myself busy all the time being up to no good. And then at breakfast time on Saturday morning, the morning of the outing, I found a note on the kitchen table. It said, "There's some eggs in the pantry. Take your boots off before you go to bed." My uncle's wife had gone, as quick as a flash.

When my uncle saw the note, he tugged out the flag of his handkerchief and blew such a hubbub of trumpets that the plates on the dresser shook. "It's the same every year," he said. And then he looked at me. "But this year it's different. *You'll* have to come on the outing, too, and what the members will say I dare not think."

The charabanc drew up outside, and when the members of the outing saw my uncle and me squeeze out of the shop together, both of us cat-licked and brushed in our Sunday best, they snarled like a zoo.

"Are you bringing a *boy?*" asked Mr. Benjamin Franklyn as we climbed into the charabanc. He looked at me with horror.

"Boys is nasty," said Mr. Weazley.

"He hasn't paid his contributions," Will Sentry said.

"No room for boys. Boys get sick in charabancs."

"So do you, Enoch Davies," said my uncle.

"Might as well bring *women*."

They way they said it, women were worse than boys.

"Better than bringing grandfathers."

"Grandfathers is nasty too," said Mr. Weazley.

"What can we do with him when we stop for refreshments?"

"I'm a grandfather," said Mr. Weazley.

"Twenty-six minutes to opening time," shouted an old man in a panama hat, not looking at a watch. They forgot me at once.

"Good old Mr. Cadwalladwr," they cried, and the charabanc started off down the village street.

A few cold women stood at their doorways, grimly watching us go. A very small boy waved goodbye, and his mother boxed his ears. It was a beautiful August morning.

We were out of the village, and over the bridge, and up the hill toward Steeplehat Wood when Mr. Franklyn, with his list of names in his hand, called out loud, "Where's old O. Jones?"

"Where's old O.?"

"We've left old O. behind."

"Can't go without old O."

And though Mr. Weazley hissed all the way, we turned and drove back to the village, where, outside the Prince of Wales, old O. Jones was waiting patiently and alone with a canvas bag.

"I didn't want to come at all," old O. Jones said as they hoisted him into the charabranc and clapped him on the back and pushed him on a seat and stuck a bottle in his hand, "but I always go." And over the bridge and up the hill and under the deep green wood and along the dusty road we wove, slow cows and ducks flying by, until "Stop the bus!" Mr. Weazley cried, "I left my teeth on the mantelpiece,"

"Never you mind," they said, "you're not going to bite nobody," and they gave him a bottle with a straw.

"I might want to smile," he said.

"Not you," they said.

"What's the time, Mr. Cadwalladwr?"

"Twelve minutes to go," shouted back the old man in the panama, and they all began to curse him.

The charabanc pulled up outside the Mountain Sheep, a small, unhappy public house with a thatched roof like a wig with ringworm. From a flagpole by the Gents fluttered the flag of Siam. I knew it was the flag of Siam because of cigarette cards. The landlord stood at the door to welcome us, simpering like a wolf. He was a long, lean, black-fanged man with a greased love-curl and pouncing eyes. "What a beautiful August day!" he said, and touched his love-curl with a claw. That was the way he must have welcomed the Mountain Sheep before he ate it, I said to myself. The members rushed out, bleating, and into the bar.

"You keep an eye on the charra," my uncle said, "see nobody steals it now."

"There's nobody to steal it," I said, "except some cows," but my uncle was gustily blowing his bugle in the bar. I looked at the cows opposite, and they looked at me. There was nothing else for us to do. Forty-five minutes passed, like a very slow cloud. The sun shone down on the lonely road, the lost, unwanted boy, and the lake-eyed cows. In the dark bar they were so happy they were breaking glasses. A Shoni-Onion Breton man, with a beret and a necklace of onions, bicycled down the road and stopped at the door.

"*Quelle un grand matin, monsieur,*" I said.

"There's French, boy bach!" he said.

I followed him down the passage, and peered into the bar. I could hardly recognize the members of the outing. They had all changed color. Beetroot, rhubarb and puce, they hollered and rollicked in that dark, damp hole like enormous ancient bad boys, and my uncle surged in the middle, all red whiskers and bellies. On the floor was broken glass and Mr. Weazley.

"Drinks all round," cried Bob the Fiddle, a small, absconding man with bright blue eyes and a plump smile.

"Who's been robbing the orphans?"

"Who sold his little babby to the gyppoes?"

"Trust old Bob, he'll let you down."

"You will have your little joke," said Bob the Fiddle, smiling like a razor, "but I forgive you, boys."

Out of the fug and babel I heard: "Where's old O. Jones?" "Where are you old O.?" "He's in the kitchen cooking his dinner." "He never forgets his dinner time." "Good old O. Jones." "Come out and fight." "No, not now, later." "No, now when I'm in a temper." "Look at Will Sentry, he's proper snobbled." "Look at his willful feet." "Look at Mr. Weazley lording it on the floor."

Mr. Weazley got up, hissing like a gander. "That boy pushed me down deliberate," he said, pointing to me at the door, and I slunk away down the passage and out to the mild, good cows.

Time clouded over, the cows wondered, I threw a stone at them and they wandered, wondering, away. Then out blew my Uncle, ballooning, and one by one the members lumbered after him in a grizzle. They had drunk the Mountain Sheep dry. Mr. Weazley had won a string of onions that the Shoni-Onion man had raffled in the bar.

"What's the good of onions if you left your teeth on the mantelpiece?" he said. And when I looked through the back window of the thundering charabanc, I saw the pub grow smaller in the distance. And the flag of Siam, from the flagpole by the Gents, fluttered now at half mast.

The Blue Bull, the Dragon, the Star of Wales, the Twll in the Wall, the Sour Grapes, the Shepherd's Arms, the Bells of Aberdovey: I had nothing to do in the whole wild August world but remember the names where the outing stopped and keep an eye on the charabanc. And whenever it passed a public house, Mr. Weazley would cough like a billy goat and cry, "Stop the bus, I'm dying of breath." And back we would all have to go.

Closing time meant nothing to the members of that outing. Behind locked doors, they hymned and rumpused all the beautiful afternoon. And, when a policeman entered the Druid's Tap by the back door, and found them all choral with beer, "Sssh!" said Noah Bowen, "the pub is shut."

"Where do you come from?" he said in his buttoned, blue voice.

They told him.

"I got a auntie there," the policeman said. And very soon he was singing "Asleep in the Deep."

Off we drove again at last, the charabanc bouncing with tenors and flagons, and came to a river that rushed along among willows.

"Water!" they shouted.

"Porthcawl!" sang my uncle.

"Where's the donkeys?" said Mr. Weazley.

And out they lurched, to paddle and whoop in the cool,

white, winding water. Mr. Franklyn, trying to polka on the slippery stones, fell in twice. "Nothing is simple," he said with dignity as he oozed up the bank.

"It's cold!" they cried.

"It's lovely!"

"It's smooth as a moth's nose!"

"It's *better* than Porthcawl!"

And dusk came down warm and gentle on thirty wild, wet, pickled, splashing men without a care in the world at the end of the world in the west of Wales. And, "Who goes there?" called Will Sentry to a wild duck flying.

They stopped at the Hermit's Nest for a rum to keep out the cold. "I played for Aberavon in 1898," said a stranger to Enoch Davies.

"Liar," said Enoch Davies.

"I can show you photos," said the stranger.

"Forged," said Enoch Davies.

"And I'll show you my cap at home."

"Stolen."

"I got friends to prove it," the stranger said in a fury.

"Bribed," said Enoch Davies.

On the way home, through the simmering moon-splashed dark, old O. Jones began to cook his supper on a primus stove in the middle of the charabanc. Mr. Weazley coughed himself blue in the smoke. "Stop the bus!" he cried, "I'm dying of breath." We all climbed down into the moonlight. There was not a public house in sight. So they carried out the remaining cases, and the primus stove, and old O. Jones himself, and took them into a field, and sat down in a circle in the field and drank and sang while old O. Jones cooked sausage and mash and the moon flew above us. And there I drifted to sleep against my uncle's mountainous waistcoat, and, as I slept, "Who goes there?" called out Will Sentry to the flying moon.

(1953)

THE CRUMBS OF ONE MAN'S YEAR

Slung as though in a hammock, or a lull, between one Christmas forever over and a New Year nearing full of relentless surprises, waywardly and gladly I pry back at those wizening twelve months and see only a waltzing snippet of the tipsy-turvy times, flickers of vistas, flashes of queer fishes, patches and chequers of a bard's-eye view.

Of what is coming in the New Year I know nothing, except that all that is certain will come like thunderclaps or like comets in the shape of four-leaved clovers, and that all that is unforeseen will appear with the certainty of the sun who every morning shakes a leg in the sky. And of what has gone I know only shilly-shally snatches and freckled plaids, flecks and dabs, dazzle and froth; a simple second caught in coursing snow-light; an instant, gay or sorry, struck motionless in the curve of flight like a bird or a scythe; the spindrift leaf and stray-paper whirl, canter, quarrel and people-chase of everybody's street; suddenly the way the grotesque wind slashes and freezes at a corner the clothes of a passerby so that she stays remembered, cold and still until the world like a night light in a nursery goes out; and a waddling couple of the small occurrences, comic as ducks, that quack their way through our calamitous days; whits and dots and tittles.

"Look back, back," the big voices clarion, "look back at the black colossal year," while the rich music fanfares and dead-marches.

I can give you only a scattering of some of the crumbs of one man's year, and the penny music whistles.

Any memory, of the long, revolving year, will do, to begin with.

I was walking, one afternoon in August, along a riverbank, thinking the same thoughts that I always think when I walk along a riverbank in August. As I was walking, I was thinking—now it is August and I am walking along a riverbank. I do not think I was thinking of anything else. I should have been thinking of what I should have been doing, but I was thinking only of what I was doing then and it was all right: it was good, and ordinary, and slow, and idle, and old, and sure, and what I was doing I could have been doing a thousand years before, had I been alive then and myself or any other man. You could have thought the river was ringing—almost you could hear the green, rapid bells sing in it: it could have been the River Elusina, "that dances at the noise of Musick, for with Musick it bubbles, dances and grows sandy, and so continues til the musick ceases. . ."; or it could have been the River "in Judea that runs swiftly all the six dayes of the week, and stands still and rests all their Sabbath." There were trees blowing, standing still, growing, knowing, whose names I never knew. (Once, indeed, with a friend I wrote a poem beginning "All trees are oaks, except fir trees.") There were birds being busy, or sleep-flying, in the sky. (The poem had continued, "All birds are robins, except crows, or rooks.") Nature was doing what it was doing, and thinking just that. And I was walking and thinking that I was walking, and for August it was not such a cold day. And then I saw, drifting along the water, a piece of paper, and I thought: something wonderful may be written on this paper. I was alone on the gooseberry earth, or alone for two green miles, and a message drifted towards me on that tabby-coloured water that ran through the middle of the cow-patched, mooing field. It was a message from multitudinous nowhere to my solitary self. I put out my stick and caught the piece of paper and held it close to the riverbank. It was a page torn from a very old periodical. That I could see. I leant over and read, through water, the message on the rippling page. I made out, with difficulty, only one sentence: it commemorated the fact that, over a hundred years ago, a man in Worcester had, for a bet, eaten at one sitting fifty-two pounds of plums.

And any other memory, of the long evolving year, will do, to go on with.

Here now, to my memory, come peacefully blitz and pieces of the Fifth of November, guys in the streets and forks in the sky, when Catherine wheels and Jacky jumps and good bombs burst in the blistered areas. The rockets are few but they star between roofs and up to the wall of the warless night. "A penny for the Guy?" "No, that's my father." The great joke brocks and sizzles. Sirius explodes in the back yard by the shelter. Timorous ladies sit in their back rooms, with the eighth programme on very loud. Retiring men snarl under their blankets. In the unkempt gardens of the very rich, the second butler lights a squib. In everybody's street the fearless children shout, under the little, homely raids. But I was standing on a signalling country hill where they fed a hungry bonfire Guy with brushwood, sticks and crackerjacks; the bonfire Guy whooped for more; small sulphurous puddings banged in his burning belly, and his thorned hair caught. He lurched, and made common noises. He was a long time dying on the hill over the starlit fields where the tabby river, without a message, ran on, with bells and trout and tins and bangles and literature and cats in it, to the sea never out of sound.

And on one occasion, in this long dissolving year, I remember that I boarded a London bus from a district I have forgotten, and where I certainly could have been up to little good, to an appointment that I did not want to keep.

It was a shooting green spring morning, nimble and crocus, with all the young women treading on naked flower-stalks, the metropolitan sward, swinging their milkpail handbags, gentle, fickle, inviting, accessible, forgiving each robustly abandoned gesture of salutation before it was made or imagined, assenting, as they revelled demurely towards the manicure salon or the typewriting office, to all the ardent unspoken endearments of shaggy strangers and the winks and pipes of cloven-footed sandwichmen. The sun shrilled, the buses gambolled, policemen and daffodils bowed in the breeze that tasted of buttermilk. Delicate carousal plashed and babbled from the public houses which were not yet open. I felt like a young god. I removed my collar studs and opened my shirt. I tossed back my hair. There was an aviary in my heart but without any owls or eagles. My cheeks were cherried warm, I smelt, I thought, of sea pinks. To the sound of madrigals sung by slim sopranos in waterfalled valleys where I was the only tenor, I leapt on to a bus. The bus was full. Carefree, open-collared, my eyes alight, my veins full of the spring as a dancer's shoe should be full of champagne, I stood, in love and at ease and always young, on the packed lower deck. And a man of exactly my own age—or perhaps he was a little older—got up and offered me his seat. He said, in a respectful voice, as though to an old justice of the peace, "Please, won't you take my seat?" and then he added—"Sir."

How many variegations of inconsiderable defeats and dis-illusionments I have forgotten! How many shades and shapes from the polychromatic zebra house! How many Joseph's coats I have left uncalled-for in the Gentlemen's Cloakrooms of the year!

And one man's year is like the country of a cloud, mapped on the sky, that soon will vanish into the watery, ordered wastes, into the spinning rule, into the dark which is light. Now the cloud is flying, very slowly, out of sight, and I can remember of all that voyaging geography, no palaced morning hills or huge plush valleys in the downing sun, forgets simmering with birds, stagged moors, merry legendary meadowland, bullish plains, but only—the street near Waterloo Station where a small boy, wear-ing cut-down khaki and a steel helmet, pushed a pram full of fire-wood and shouted, in a dispassionate voice, after each passer-by, "Where's your tail?"

The estuary pool under the collapsed castle, where the July children rolled together in original mud, skreaking and yauping, and low life, long before newts, twitched on their hands.

The crisp path through the field in this December snow, in the deep dark, where we trod the buried grass like ghosts on dry toast.

The single-line run along the spring-green riverbank where water-voles went Indian file to work, and where the young im-patient voles, in their sleek vests, always in a hurry, jumped over the threadbare backs of the old ones.

The razor-scarred back-street café bar where a man with cut cheeks and chewed ears, huskily and furiously complained, over tarry tea, that the new baby panda in the Zoo was not floodlit.

The gully sands in March, under the flayed and flailing cliff-top trees, when the wind played old Harry, or old Thomas, with me, and cormorants, far off, sped like motorboats across the bay, as I weaved towards the toppling town and the black, loud Lion where the cat, who purred like a fire, looked out of two cinders at the gently swilling retired sea-captains in the snug-as-a-bug back bar.

And the basement kitchen in nipping February, with napkins on the line slung across from door to chockablock corner, and a bicycle by the larder very much down at wheels, and hats and toy engines and bottles and spanners on the broken rocking chair, and billowing papers and half-finished crosswords stacked on the radio always turned full tilt, and the fire smoking, and onions peeling, and chips always spitting on the stove, and small men in their overcoats talking of self-discipline and the ascetic life until the air grew woodbine-blue and the clock choked and the traffic died.

And then the moment of a night in that cavorting spring, rare and unforgettable as a bicycle clip found in the middle of the desert. The lane was long and soused and dark that led to the house I helped to fill and bedraggle.

"Who's left this in this corner?"

"What, where?"

"Here, this."

A doll's arm, the chitterlings of a clock, a saucepan full of hatbands.

The lane was rutted as though by bosky water carts, and so dark you couldn't see your front in spite of you. Rain barrelled down. On one side you couldn't hear the deer that lived there, and on the other side—voices began to whisper, muffled in the midnight sack. A man's voice and a woman's voice. "Lovers," I said to myself. For at night the heart comes out, like a cat on the tiles. Discourteously I shone my torch. There, in the thick rain, a young man and a young woman stood, very close together, near the hedge that whirred in the wind. And a yard from them, another young man sat staidly, on the grass verge, holding an open book from which he appeared to read. And in the very rutted and puddly middle of the lane, two dogs were fighting, with brutish concentration and in absolute silence.

(1946)

LAUGHARNE

Off and on, up and down, high and dry, man and boy, I've been living now for fifteen years, or centuries, in this timeless, beautiful, barmy (both spellings) town, in this far, forgetful, important place of herons, cormorants (known here as billy duckers), castle, churchyard, gulls, ghosts, geese, feuds, scares, scandals, cherry trees, mysteries, jackdaws in the chimneys, bats in the belfry, skeletons in the cupboards, pubs, mud, cockles, flatfish, curlews, rain, and human, often all too human, beings; and, though still very much a foreigner, I am hardly ever stoned in the streets any more, and can claim to be able to call several of the inhabitants, and a few of the herons, by their Christian names.

Now, some people live in Laugharne because they were born in Laugharne and saw no good reason to move; others migrated here, for a number of curious reasons, from places as distant and improbable as Tonypandy or even England, and have now been absorbed by the natives; some entered the town in the dark and immediately disappeared, and can sometimes be heard, on hushed black nights, making noises in ruined houses, or perhaps it is the white owls breathing close together, like ghosts in bed; others have almost certainly come here to escape the international police, or their wives; and there are those, too, who still do not know, and will never know, why they are here at all: you can see them, any day of the week, slowly, dopily, wandering up and down the streets like Welsh opium-eaters, half-asleep in a heavy bewildered daze. And some, like myself, just came, one day, for the day, and never left; got off the bus, and forgot to get on again. Whatever the reason, if any, for our being here, in this timeless, mild, beguiling island of a town with its seven public houses, one chapel in action, one church, one factory, two billiard tables, one St. Bernard (without brandy), one policeman, three rivers, a visiting sea, one Rolls-Royce selling fish and chips, one cannon (cast-iron), one chancellor (flesh and blood), one portreeve, one Danny Raye, and a multitude of mixed birds, here we just are, and there is nowhere like it anywhere at all.

But when you say, in a nearby village or town, that you come from this unique, this waylaying, old, lost Laugharne where some people start to retire before they start to work and where longish journeys, of a few hundred yards, are often undertaken only on bicycles, then, oh! the wary edging away, the whispers and whimpers, and nudges, the swift removal of portable objects:

"Let's get away while the going is good," you hear.

"Laugharne's where they quarrel with boat hooks."

"All the women there's got webfeet."

"Mind out for the Evil Eye!"

"Never go there at the full moon!"

They are only envious. They envy Laugharne its minding of its own, strange, business; its sane disregard for haste; its generous acceptance of the follies of others, having so many, ripe and piping, of its own; its insular, feather-bed air; its philosophy of "It will all be the same in a hundred years' time." They deplore its right to be, in their eyes, so wrong, and to enjoy it so much as well. And, through envy and indignation, they label and libel it a legendary lazy little black-magical bedlam by the sea. And is it? Of *course not,* I hope.

(*1953*)

RETURN JOURNEY

NARRATOR: It was a cold white day in High Street, and nothing to stop the wind slicing up from the Docks; for where the squat and tall shops had shielded the town from the sea lay their blitzed flat graves marbled with snow and headstoned with fences. Dogs, delicate as cats on water, as though they had gloves on their paws, padded over the vanished buildings. Boys romped, calling high and clear, on top of a levelled chemist's and a shoe-shop; and a little girl, wearing a man's cap, threw a snowball in a chill deserted garden that had once been the Jug and Bottle of the Prince of Wales. The wind cut up the street with a soft sea-noise hanging on its arm, like a hooter in a muffler. I could see the swathed hill stepping up out of the town, which you never could see properly before, and the powdered fields of the roofs of Milton Terrace and Watkin Street and Fullers Row. Fish-frailed, netbagged, umbrella'd, pixie-capped, fur-shoed, blue-nosed, puce-lipped, blinkered like drayhorses, scarved, mittened, goloshed, wearing everything but the cat's blanket, crushes of shopping women crunched in the little Lapland of the once grey drab street, blew and queued and yearned for hot tea, as I began my search through Swansea town cold and early on that wicked February morning. I went into the hotel. "Good morning."

The hall-porter did not answer. I was just another snowman to him. He did not know that I was looking for someone after fourteen years, and he did not care. He stood and shuddered, staring through the glass of the hotel door at the snowflakes sailing down the sky, like Siberan confetti. The bar was just opening, but already one customer puffed and shook at the counter with a full pint of half-frozen Tawe water in his wrapped-up hand. I said "Good morning," and the barmaid, polishing the counter vigorously, as though it were a rare and valuable piece of Swansea china, said to her first customer:

BARMAID: Seen the film at the Elysium Mr. Griffiths there's snow isn't it did you come up on your bicycle our pipes burst Monday . . .

NARRATOR: A pint of bitter, please.

BARMAID: Proper little lake in the kitchen got to wear your Wellingtons when you boil a egg one and four please . . .

CUSTOMER: The cold gets me just here . . .

BARMAID: . . . and eightpence change that's your liver Mr. Griffiths you been on the cocoa again . . .

NARRATOR: I wonder whether you remember a friend of mine? He always used to come to this bar, some years ago. Every morning, about this time.

CUSTOMER: Just by here it gets me. I don't know what'd happen if I didn't wear a band . . .

BARMAID: What's his name?

NARRATOR: Young Thomas.

BARMAID: Lots of Thomases come here it's a kind of home from home for Thomases isn't it Mr. Griffiths what's he look like?

NARRATOR [*slowly*]: He'd be about seventeen or eighteen . . .

BARMAID: . . . I was seventeen once . . .

NARRATOR: . . . and above medium height. Above medium height for Wales, I mean, he's five foot six and a half. Thick blubber lips; snub nose; curly mouse-brown hair; one front tooth broken after playing a game called cats and dogs in the Mermaid, Mumbles; speaks rather fancy; truculent; plausible; a bit of a shower-off; plus fours and no breakfast, you know; used to have poems printed in the *Herald of Wales*; there was one about an open-air performance of *Electra* in Mrs. Bertie Perkins' garden in Sketty; lived up the Uplands; a bombastic adolescent provincial bohemian with a thick-knotted artist's tie made out of his sister's scarf—she never knew where it had gone—and a cricket-shirt dyed bottle-green; a gabbing, ambitious, mock-tough, pretentious young man; and mole-y, too.

BARMAID: There's words what d'you want to find *him* for I wouldn't touch him with a bargepole . . . would you, Mr. Griffiths? Mind, you can never tell. I remember a man came here with a monkey. Called for 'alf for himself and a pint for the monkey. And he wasn't Italian at all. Spoke Welsh like a preacher.

NARRATOR: The bar was filling up. Snowy business bellies pressed their watch chains against the counter; black business bowlers, damp and white now as Christmas puddings in their cloths, bobbed in front of the misty mirrors. The voice of commerce rang sternly through the lounge.

FIRST VOICE: Cold enough for you?

SECOND VOICE: How's your pipes, Mr. Lewis?

THIRD VOICE: Another winter like this'll put paid to me, Mr. Evans.

FOURTH VOICE: I got the flu . . .

FIRST VOICE: Make it a double . . .

SECOND VOICE: Similar . . .

BARMAID: Okay, baby . . .

CUSTOMER [*confidentially*]: I seem to remember a chap like you described. There couldn't be two like him let's hope. He used to work as a reporter. Down the Three Lamps I used to see him. Lifting his ikkle elbow.

NARRATOR: What's the Three Lamps like now?

CUSTOMER: It isn't like anything. It isn't there. It's nothing mun. You remember Ben Evans' stores? It's right next door to that. Ben Evans isn't there either . . .

[*Fade.*]

NARRATOR: I went out of the hotel into the snow and walked down High Street, past the flat white wastes where all the shops had been. Eddershaw Furnishers, Curry's Bicycles, Donegal Clothing Company, Doctor Scholl's, Burton Tailors, W. H. Smith, Boots Cash Chemists, Leslie's Stores, Upson's Shoes, Prince of Wales, Tucker's Fish, Stead and Simpson—all the shops bombed and vanished. Past the hole in space where Hodges and Clothiers had been, down Castle Street, past the remembered, invisible shops, Price's Fifty Shilling, and Crouch the Jeweller, Potter Gilmore Gowns, Evans Jeweller, Master's Outfitters, Style and Mantle, Lennard's Boots, True Form, Kardomah, R. E. Jones,

Dean's Tailors, David Evans, Gregory Confectioners, Bovega, Burton's, Lloyd's Bank and nothing. And into Temple Street. There the Three Lamps had stood, old Mac magisterial in his corner. And there the Young Thomas I was searching for used to stand at the counter on Friday paynights with Freddie Farr, Half Hook, Bill Latham, Cliff Williams, Gareth Hughes, Eric Hughes, Glyn Lowry, a man among men, his hat at a rakish angle, in that snug, smug, select, Edwardian holy of best-bitter holies . . .

[*Bar noises in background.*]

OLD REPORTER: Remember when I took you down the mortuary for the first time, Young Thomas? He'd never seen a corpse before, boys, except old Ron on a Saturday night. "If you want to be a proper newspaperman," I said, "you got to be well known in the right circles. You got to be *persona grata* in the mortuary, see." He went pale green, mun.

FIRST YOUNG REPORTER: Look, he's blushing now . . .

OLD REPORTER: And when we got there, what d'you think? The decorators were in at the mortuary, giving the old home a bit of a re-do like. Up on ladders having a slap at the roof. Young Thomas didn't see 'em; he had his popeyes glued on the slab, and when one of the painters up the ladder said "Good morning, gents" in a deep voice, he upped in the air and out of the place like a ferret. Laugh!

BARMAID [*off*]: You've had enough, Mr. Roberts. You heard what I said.

[*Noise of a gentle scuffle.*]

SECOND YOUNG REPORTER [*casually*]: There goes Mr. Roberts.

OLD REPORTER: Well fair do's they throw you out very genteel in this pub . . .

FIRST YOUNG REPORTER: Ever seen Young Thomas covering a soccer match down the Vetch and working it out in tries?

SECOND YOUNG REPORTER: And up the Mannesman Hall shouting "Good footwork, sir," and a couple of punch-drunk colliers galumphing about like jumbos.

FIRST YOUNG REPORTER: What you been reporting today, Young Thomas?

SECOND YOUNG REPORTER: Two-typewriter Thomas the ace news-dick . . .

OLD REPORTER: Let's have a dekko at your notebook. "Called at British Legion. Nothing. Called at Hospital. One broken leg. Auction at the Metropole. Ring Mr. Beynon *re* Gymanfa Ganu. Lunch. Pint and pasty at the Singleton with Mrs. Giles. Bazaar at Bethesda Chapel. Chimney on fire at Tontine Street. Walters Road Sunday School Outing. Rehearsal of the *Mikado* at Skewen" —all front-page stuff . . .

[*Fade.*]

NARRATOR: The voices of fourteen years ago hung silent in the snow and ruin, and in the falling winter morning I walked on through the white havoc'd centre where once a very young man I knew had mucked about as chirpy as a sparrow after the sips and titbits and small change of the town. Near the *Evening Post* building and the fragment of the Castle, I stopped a man whose face I thought I recognised from a long time ago. I said: I wonder if you can tell me . . .

PASSER-BY: Yes?

NARRATOR: He peered out of his blanketing scarves and from under his snowballed balaclava like an Eskimo with a bad conscience. I said: If you can tell me whether you used to know a chap called Young Thomas. He worked on the *Post* and used to wear an overcoat sometimes with the check lining inside out so that you could play giant draughts on him. He wore a conscious woodbine, too . . .

PASSER-BY: What d'you mean, conscious woodbine?

NARRATOR: . . . and a perched pork-pie with a peacock feather, and he tried to slouch like a newshawk even when he was attending a meeting of the Gorseinon Buffalos . . .

PASSER-BY: Oh, *him!* He owes me half a crown. I haven't seen him since the old Kardomah days. He wasn't a reporter then; he'd just left the Grammar School. Him and Charlie Fisher—

Charlie's got whiskers now—and Tom Warner and Fred Janes, drinking coffee-dashes arguing the toss.

NARRATOR: What about?

PASSER-BY: Music and poetry and painting and politics. Einstein and Epstein, Stravinsky and Greta Garbo, death and religion, Picasso and girls . . .

NARRATOR: And then?

PASSER-BY: Communism, symbolism, Bradman, Braque, the Watch Committee, free love, free beer, murder, Michelangelo, ping-pong, ambition, Sibelius and girls . . .

NARRATOR: Is that all?

PASSER-BY: How Dan Jones was going to compose the most prodigious symphony, Fred Janes paint the most miraculously meticulous picture, Charlie Fisher catch the poshest trout, Vernon Watkins and Young Thomas write the most boiling poems, how they would ring the bells of London and paint it like a tart . . .

NARRATOR: And after that?

PASSER-BY: Oh, the hissing of the butt-ends in the drains of the coffee-dashes and the tinkle and the gibble-gabble of the morning young lounge lizards as they talked about Augustus John, Emil Jannings, Carnera, Dracula, Amy Johnson, trial marriage, pocket money, the Welsh sea, the London stars, King Kong, anarchy, darts, T. S. Eliot and girls . . . Diw, it's cold!

NARRATOR: And he hurried on, into the dervish snow, without a good morning or goodbye, swaddled in his winter woollens like a man in the island of his deafness, and I felt that perhaps he had never stopped at all to tell me of one more departed stage in the progress of the boy I was pursuing. The Kardomah Café was razed to the snow, the voices of the coffee-drinkers—poets, painters, and musicians in their beginnings—lost in the willynilly flying of the years and the flakes.

Down College Street I walked then, past the remembered invisible shops, Langley's, Castle Cigar Co., T. B. Brown, Pullar's, Aubrey Jeremiah, Goddard Jones, Richards, Hornes, Marles, Pleasance and Harper, Star Supply, Sidney Heath,

Wesley Chapel and nothing. . . . My search was leading me back, through pub and job and café, to the school.

[*Fade. School bell.*]

SCHOOLMASTER: Oh yes, yes, I remember him well,
though I do not know if I would recognise him now:
nobody grows any younger, or better,
and boys grow into much the sort of men one would suppose
though sometimes the mustaches bewilder
and one finds it hard to reconcile one's memory of a small
none-too-clean urchin lying his way unsuccessfully out of his
    homework
with a fierce and many-medalled sergeant-major with three children
    or a divorced chartered accountant;
and it is hard to realise
that some little tousled rebellious youth whose only claim
to fame among his contemporaries was his undisputed right
to the championship of the spitting contest
is now perhaps one's own bank manager.
Oh yes, I remember him well, the boy you are searching for:
he looked like most boys, no better, brighter, or more respectful:
he cribbed, mitched, spilt ink, rattled his desk and
garbled his lessons with the worst of them;
he could smudge, hedge, smirk, wriggle, wince,
whimper, blarney, badger, blush, deceive, be
devious, stammer, improvise, assume
offended dignity or righteous indignation as though to the manner
    born;
sullenly and reluctantly he drilled, for some small
crime, under Sergeant Bird, so wittily nicknamed
Oiseau, on Wednesday half-holidays,
appeared regularly in detention classes,
hid in the cloakroom during algebra,
was, when a newcomer, thrown into the brushes of the
lower playground by bigger boys,
and threw newcomers into the bushes of the lower
playground when *he* was a bigger boy;
he scuffled at prayers,
he interpolated, smugly, the time-honoured wrong
irreverent words into the morning hymns,

he helped to damage the headmaster's rhubarb,
was thirty-third in trigonometry,
and, as might be expected, edited the school magazine.

[*Fade.*]

NARRATOR: The hall is shattered, the echoing corridors charred where he scribbled and smudged and yawned in the long green days, waiting for the bell and the scamper into the yard; the school on Mount Pleasant Hill has changed its face and its ways. Soon, they say, it may be no longer the school at all he knew and loved when he was a boy up to no good but the beat of his blood; the names are havoc'd from the hall and the carved initials burned from the broken wood. But the names remain. What names did he know of the dead? Who of the honoured dead did he know such a long time ago? The names of the dead in the living heart and head remain forever. Of all the dead whom did he know?

[*Funeral Bell.*]

VOICE: Evans, K. J., Haines, G. C., Roberts, I. L., Moxham, J., Thomas, H., Baines, W., Bazzard. F. H., Beer, L. J., Bucknell, R., Twford, G., Vagg, E. A., Wright, G.

[*Fade.*]

NARRATOR: Then I tacked down the snowblind hill, a cat-o'-nine-gales whipping from the sea, and, white and eiderdowned in the smothering flurry, people padded past me up and down like prowling featherbeds. And I plodded through the ankle-high one cloud that foamed the town, into flat Gower Street, its buildings melted, and along long Helen's Road. Now my search was leading me back to the seashore.

[*Noise of sea, softly.*]

NARRATOR: Only two living creatures stood on the promenade, near the cenotaph, facing the tossed crystal sea: a man in a chewed muffler and a ratting cap, and an angry dog of a mixed make. The man diddered in the cold, beat his bare blue hands together, waited for some sign from sea or snow; the dog shouted at the weather, and fixed his bloodshot eyes on Mumbles Head. But when the man and I talked together, the dog piped down and fixed his eyes on me, blaming me for the snow. The man spoke towards the sea. Year in, year out, whatever the weather, once in the daytime, once in the dark, he always came to look at the sea. He knew all the dogs and boys and old men who came to see the sea, who ran or gambolled on the sand or stooped at the edges of the waves as though over a wild, wide, rolling ashcan. He knew the lovers who went to lie in the sandhills, the striding masculine women who roared at their terriers like tiger tamers, the loafing men whose work it was in the world to observe the great employment of the sea. He said:

PROMENADE-MAN: Oh yes, yes, I remember him well, but I didn't know what was his name. I don't know the names of none of the sandboys. They don't know mine. About fourteen or fifteen years old, you said, with a little red cap. And he used to play by Vivian's Stream. He used to dawdle in the arches, you said, and lark about on the railway lines and holler at the old sea. He'd mooch about the dunes and watch the tankers and the tugs and the banana boats come out of the Docks. He was going to run away to sea, he said. *I* know. On Saturday afternoon he'd go down to the sea when it was a long way out, and hear the foghorns though he couldn't see the ships. And on Sunday nights, after chapel, he'd be swaggering with his pals along the prom, whistling after the girls.

[*Titter.*]

GIRL: Does your mother know you're out? Go away now. Stop following us.

[*Another girl titters.*]

GIRL: Don't you say nothing, Hetty, you're only encouraging. No thank *you,* Mr. Cheeky, with your cut-glass accent and your father's trilby! I don't want *no* walk on *no* sands. What d'you say? Ooh, listen to him, Het, he's swallowed a dictionary. No, I don't want to go with nobody up no lane in the moonlight, see, and I'm not a baby-snatcher neither. I seen you going to school along Terrace Road, Mr. Glad-Eye, with your little satchel and wearing your red cap and all. You seen me wearing my . . . no you never. Hetty, mind your glasses! Hetty Harris, you're as bad as them. Oh, go away and do your homework, you. No I'm not then. I'm nobody's homework, see. Cheek! Hetty Harris, don't you let him! Oooh, there's brazen! Well, just to the end of the prom, if you like. No further, mind . . .

PROMENADE-MAN: Oh yes, I knew him well. I've known him by the thousands . . .

NARRATOR: Even now, on the frozen foreshore, a high, far cry of boys, all like the boy I sought, slid on the glass of the streams and snowballed each other and the sky. Then I went on my way from the sea, up Brynmill Terrace and into Glanbrydan Avenue where Bert Trick had kept a grocer's shop and, in the kitchen, threatened the annihilation of the ruling classes over sandwiches and jelly and blancmange. And I came to the shops and houses of the Uplands. Here and around here it was that the journey had begun of the one I was pursuing through his past.

[*Old piano cinema-music in the background.*]

FIRST VOICE: Here was once the flea-pit picture-house where he whooped for the scalping Indians with Jack Basset and banged for the rustler's guns.

NARRATOR: Jackie Basset, killed.

THIRD VOICE: Here once was Mrs. Ferguson's, who sold the best gob-stoppers and penny packets full of surprises and a sweet kind of glue.

FIRST VOICE: In the fields behind Cwmdonkin Drive, the Murrays chased him and all cats.

SECOND VOICE: No fires now where the outlaws' fires burned and the paradisiacal potatoes roasted in the embers.

THIRD VOICE: In the Craig beneath Town Hill he was a lonely killer hunting the wolves (or rabbits) and the red Sioux tribe (or Mitchell brothers).

[*Fade cinema-music into background of children's voices reciting, in unison, the names of the counties of Wales.*]

FIRST VOICE: In Mirador School he learned to read and count. Who made the worst raffia doilies? Who put water in Joyce's galoshes, every morning prompt as prompt? In the afternoons, when the children were good, they read aloud from *Struwwel-peter*. And when they were bad, they sat alone in the empty class-room, hearing, from above them, the distant, terrible, sad music of the late piano lesson.

[*The children's voices fade. The piano lesson continues in background.*]

NARRATOR: And I went up, through the white Grove, into Cwmdonkin Park, the snow still sailing and the childish, lonely, remembered music fingering on in the suddenly gentle wind. Dusk was folding the park around, like another, darker snow. Soon the bell would ring for the closing of the gates, though the park was empty. The park-keeper walked by the reservoir, where swans had glided, on his white rounds. I walked by his side and asked him my questions, up the swathed drives past buried beds and loaded utterly still furred and birdless trees towards the last gate. He said:

PARK-KEEPER: Oh yes, yes, I knew him well. He used to climb the reservoir railings and pelt the old swans. Run like a billygoat over the grass you should keep off of. Cut branches off the trees. Carve words on the benches. Pull up moss in the rock-ery, go snip through the dahlias. Fight in the bandstand. Climb the elms and moon up the top like a owl. Light fires in the bushes. Play on the green bank. Oh yes, I knew him well. I think he was happy all the time. I've known him by the thousands.

NARRATOR: We had reached the last gate. Dusk drew around us and the town. I said: What has become of him now?

PARK-KEEPER: Dead.

NARRATOR: The park-keeper said . . .

[*The park bell rings.*]

PARK-KEEPER: Dead . . . Dead . . . Dead . . . Dead . . . Dead . . . Dead.

(*1947*)

To begin with, a city;
a fair, grey day;
a day as lively and noisy as a close gossip of sparrows,
as terribly impersonal
as a sea cavern full of machines;
when morning is driving down from the roofs of buildings
into stone labyrinths and traffic-webs,
when each man is alone forever in the midst of the masses of men
and all the separate movements of the morning crowds
are lost together in the heartbeats of the clocks;
a day when the long noise of the sea is forgotten,
street-drowned, in another memory:
of the *sound* itself of smoke and sailing dust,
trumpets of traffic signs and hoardings and posters
rasp of the red and green signal-lights
the scraped string-voices of overhead wires
and the owlsound of the dry wind in the tube-tunnels,
the blare and ragged drumroll of the armies of pavements and
chimneys and crossings and street walls,
the riding choirs of the wheels,
the always remembered, even though continual seamusic,
music of the towers and bridges and spires and domes of the island
    city.

There is peace under one roof.

Then birds flying:
suddenly, easily, as though from another country, over and
around the still, still-living image in the dead middle of
the hit-flat, burnt-black city areas killed at night;

* Commentary by Dylan Thomas for the first two reels of a Ministry
of Information documentary film, *Our Country*, made by John Eldridge
and J. Jago (Strand Film Company).

and all the stones remember and sing the cathedral of each
blitzed dead body that lay or lies in the bomber-and-dove-
flown-over cemeteries of the dumb, heroic streets.

And the eyes of St. Paul's move over London:

to the crowds of the shunting, flagged and whistling,
cluttered eavehollow otherworld under glass and steam,
the loud-speaking terminus,
to a thousand histories of men and women on the tides of
the platform
going home now, going home to a quiet county,
going to war now, going to that strange country,
going away, coming back to the ten-million-headed city,
or going away never to come back,
going out, out
over the racing rails in a grumble of London-leaving thunder
over the mazetrack of metal through a wink and a spin of
towns and signals and fields,
out
to the edges of the explosive, the moon-moved, man-indifferent,
    capsizing sea.

The shape of another country lies so near,
the wind on Dover Cliffs could touch it with its finger.

And from this island-end, white-faced over the shifting sea-dyes,
a man may hear his country's body talking, and be caught
in the weathers of her eyes;
and, striding inland, is plunged again in the armoured floods.

And war hangs heavy, too, over the apple-dangled acres,
shadowing the small round hills of the heavy-hanging fruit;
only the fruit-loving birds flew, once, over these treetops.
But nothing under the sun can change the smiling of sun on
    harvest,
the ripeness, the sundust:
the faces of the fruit-pickers, reflected in the mirror skin
of the orchard at peace,

hold peace within them like the unkillable sweetness of
country summer.

Summer is flying along plants and flowers,
through harvest corridors, swiftly over the short country
days of women and children from city smoke;
they come like a holiday, every year, they come to work in the
    fields,
and to catch again the flying open summer in their hands and eyes;
in the airless courts and alleys at home, it must last them
a long winter
and a leafless dark spring.

A man may see
from the roads he rides
summer and war
on all four fair sides.

(1943)

PART TWO

WELSH POETS

The position—if poets must have positions, other than upright—
of the poet born in Wales or of Welsh parentage and writing his
poems in English is today made by many people unnecessarily,
and trivially, difficult. There are a number of young Welshmen
writing poems in English who, insisting passionately that they are
Welshmen, should by rights be writing in Welsh, but who, unable
to write in Welsh or reluctant to do so because of the uncom-
mercial nature of the language, often give the impression that
their writing in English is only a condescension to the influence
and ubiquity of a tyrannous foreign tongue. I do not belong to
that number.

   This is not a programme of Welsh poetry, nor of Anglo-
Welsh poetry—the latter is an ambiguous compromise. I am going
to introduce, with as little explanation and criticism as possible,
poems written in English by poets who either are Welsh by birth
or have very strong Welsh associations. I want you to consider
some of the poems in English that a small and distinguished
number of Welshmen have written—mostly in the forty-five years
of this century. I should prefer to call this an anthology with comments, rather than a brief lecture with quotations. Really, this
has to be an anthology, because, as far as I can read and understand, there is no logical thread running through the centuries of
traditional poetry in English which can be said to possess a particularly Welsh characteristic.

   There are not more than half a dozen Welsh poets who wrote
in English of any genuine importance between 1622, when Henry
Vaughan was born, and 1944, when Alun Lewis died, though
there are many able and charming writers. All I can say, and all
that the examples here can illustrate, is that Welshmen have
written, from time to time, exceedingly good poetry in English. I
should like to think that that is because they were, and are, good
poets rather than good Welshmen. It's the poetry, written in the

language which is most natural to the poet, that counts, not his continent, country, island, race, class, or political persuasion.

We begin with Henry Vaughan (1622-1695). Before him was a magnificent tradition of poetry in the Welsh language. Dafydd ap Gwilym, for instance, a contemporary of Chaucer, is thought, by most Celtic scholars, to be as good a poet. Vaughan, who belonged to a very ancient Welsh family and who was educated in England, must surely have known ap Gwilym's poems. But he certainly did not follow in the exuberant bardsmanship of that great court poet but derived, in the first place, his style and matter from George Herbert. He wrote in a time when one poet *could* derive manner and content from another and yet be original. He read, too, and loved, the poetry of John Donne, but he loved it most as he saw it reflected, and transmuted, in the work of Herbert. The world, to Vaughan, was "no less than a veil of the Eternal Spirit, whose presence may be felt in any, and the smallest part." Readers today may prefer him not as a mystical theologian but as a wonderful poet of pieces: a magician of intervals. They remember odd lines, rather than odder poems. They think, perhaps, of this, from a poem on the Grave:

> A nest of nights, a gloomy sphere,
> Where shadows thicken, and the cloud
> Sits on the Sun's brow all the year,
> And nothing moves without a shroud.

Or a single image:

> . . . stars nod and sleep
> And through the dark air spin a fiery thread.

Or, again, from the "Day-Spring":

> Early, while yet the dark was gay,
> And gilt with stars more trim than day.
> Heaven's Lily and the Earth's chaste Rose,
> The green, immortal Branch arose,
> And in a solitary place
> Bowed to his father His blessed face.

And of the many superb opening lines:

> I saw Eternity the other night,
> Like a great *Ring* of pure and endless light.

But I have chosen one whole poem, "The Night," in which the figures of his authentic and intense vision move across a wild, and yet inevitably ordered, sacred landscape.

THE NIGHT

(*John* 2:3)

> Through that pure *Virgin-shrine,*
> That sacred vail drawn o'r thy glorious noon
> That men might look and live as Glo-worms shine,
>   And face the Moon:
>   Wise *Nicodemus* saw such light
>   As made him known his God by night.
>
> Most blest believer he!
> Who in that land of darkness and blinde eyes
> Thy long expected healing wings could see,
>   When thou didst rise,
>   And what can never more be done,
>   Did at mid-night speak with the Sun!
>
> O who will tell me, where
> He found thee at that dead and silent hour!
> What hallow'd solitary ground did bear
>   So rare a flower,
>   Within whose sacred leafs did lie
>   The fulness of the Deity.
>
> No mercy-seat of gold,
> No dead and dusty *Cherub,* nor carv'd stone,
> But his own living works did my Lord hold
>   And lodge alone;
>   Where *trees* and *herbs* did watch and peep
>   And wonder, while the *Jews* did sleep.

Dear night! this worlds defeat;
The stop to busie fools; cares check and curb;
The day of Spirits; my souls calm retreat
    Which none disturb!
    Christs progress, and his prayer time;
    The hours to which high Heaven doth chime.

    Gods silent, searching flight:
When my Lords head is fill'd with dew, and all
His locks are wet with the clear drops of night;
    His still, soft call;
    His knocking time; The souls dumb watch,
    When Spirits their fair kinred catch.

    Were all my loud, evil days
Calm and unhaunted as is thy dark Tent,
Whose peace but by some *Angels* wing or voice
    Is seldom rent;
    Then I in Heaven all the long year
    Would keep, and never wander here.

    But living where the Sun
Doth all things wake, and where all mix and tyre
Themselves and others, I consent and run
    To ev'ry myre,
    And by this worlds ill-guiding light,
    Erre more then I can do by night.

    There is in God (some say)
A deep, but dazling darkness; As men here
Say it is late and dusky, because they
    See not all clear;
    O for that night! where I in him
    Might live invisible and dim.

After Vaughan there is no other considerable Welsh poet—
I needn't, I hope, explain again what I mean in this context
by Welsh poetry—until the twentieth century. (Gerard Manley
Hopkins, in the nineteenth century, was influenced by bardic
forms and measures, but cannot, I'm afraid, be included in even

the broadest survey of this kind.) Two hundred years and more pass before a Welshman comes into his own again: his own, which is the one individual world of each true poet, and the same. There were Welshmen, certainly, who rhymed in English, who wrote verse, who sometimes wrote poetry. But there was none who wrote a *poem*. Poetry is the material out of which poems are made. There was John Dyer (1700-1758) of Carmarthenshire, whose "Grongar Hill," an irregular Pindaric ode, is still remembered—if only as a name—by those who read poetry for a degree and by those who live near Grongar Hill. Dyer also wrote a blank verse epic in four books, *The Fleece,* in which he discoursed of the tending of sheep, of shearing and weaving, and of trade in woollen manufactures. We must read it together one day. Then there was Sir Lewis Morris (1833-1907), also of Carmarthenshire, who wrote nearly a thousand poems, many of them long: lyrics, idyls, tragedies; odes of welcome to the Trades' Union Congress, Swansea, 1901; triolets in ladies' albums; elegies on the deaths of statesmen. The contemporary press compared his work with the *Odyssey* and *Faust,* with "L'Allegro" and "Il Penseroso." He was lauded by Mr. Gladstone. From him you can draw the portrait of the worthiest and most popular type of Victorian professional poet.

EDWARD THOMAS

Now we come into the twentieth century. From Edward Thomas, who was killed in France in 1917, to Alun Lewis, who died in India in 1944, there sprang into life a whole new body of poetry written by Welshmen. I do not think that there was in common among these poets anything but a love of poetry and of their own country. They did not, to any marked degree, derive from the same poetical sources. Edward Thomas, for instance, was devoted, through all his pitifully short, and too often melancholy, life, to the most English work of Thomas Hardy, John Clare, the Northamptonshire peasant, and William Barnes, the Dorset poet. He loved always the rich brown stables and paddocks of the painter George Morland and the loving landscapes of "Old Crome." He loved the fields, the woods, the winding roads; he knew a thousand country things: the diamonds of rain on the grass-blades, the ghostly white parsley flower, mouse and wren and robin, each year's first violets, the missel-thrush that loves juniper, hawthorn berry, hazel-tuft, new-mown hay, the cuckoo crying over the untouched dew, churches, graveyards, farms and byres, children, wild geese, horses in the sun. In the words of Walter de la Mare, Edward Thomas was a faithful and solitary lover of the lovely that is not beloved by most of us, at much expense. And when, indeed, he was killed in Flanders, a mirror of England was shattered of so pure and true a crystal that a clearer and tenderer reflection can be found no other where than in these poems. Here is a poem of his written in Wales:

THE CHILD ON THE CLIFFS

Mother, the root of this little yellow flower
Among the stones has the taste of quinine.
Things are strange to-day on the cliff. The sun
    shines so bright,
And the grasshopper works at his sewing-machine
So hard. Here's one on my hand, mother, look;
I lie so still. There's one on your book.

But I have something to tell more strange. So leave
Your book to the grasshopper, mother dear,—
Like a green knight in a dazzling market-place,—
And listen now. Can you hear what I hear
Far out? Now and then the foam there curls
And stretches a white arm out like a girl's.

Fishes and gulls ring no bells. There cannot be
A chapel or church between here and Devon,
With fishes or gulls ringing its bell,—hark!—
Somewhere under the sea or up in heaven.
"It's the bell, my son, out in the bay
On the buoy. It does sound sweet to-day."

Sweeter I never heard, mother, no, not in all Wales.
I should like to be lying under that foam,
Dead, but able to hear the sound of the bell,
And certain that you would often come
And rest, listening happily.
I should be happy if that could be.

In 1907 a Welshman published, from the Marshalsea Prison, his first book of poems, *The Soul's Destroyer*. W. H. Davies (1871-1940) was born in Monmouthshire and apprenticed, very early, to a picture-frame maker. He tramped through America as a hobo, crossed the Atlantic many times on cattle boats, and was a pedlar and street singer in England. Utterly poor and alone, educated by chance reading in the slums of great cities, he began, suddenly, to write verse which was in the direct tradition of Robert Herrick. From the very beginning to the end, during which he wrote voluminously, his poems were always fresh and simple and assured. There was inevitability in his slightest verses; unique observation in his tiniest reflections on the natural world.

His most famous poems are about birds and clouds and animals, the journeying of the planets and the seasons, the adventure of the coming and going of simple night and day. But I have chosen two of his more unfamiliar poems, which will perhaps show him, to many, in a strange new light, but in a light no less scrupulously fair and loving than that in which his kingfishers, his robin redbreasts, the little hunchbacks in the snow, all the inhabitants of his small and pure world move about their mysterious errands in the sky and on the earth he so much loved.

THE INQUEST

I took my oath I would inquire,
  Without affection, hate, or wrath,
Into the death of Ada Wright—
  So help me God! I took that oath.

When I went out to see the corpse,
  The four months' babe that died so young,
I judged it was seven pounds in weight,
  And little more than one foot long.

One eye, that had a yellow lid,
  Was shut—so was the mouth, that smiled;
The left eye open, shining bright—
  It seemed a knowing little child.

For as I looked at that one eye,
   It seemed to laugh, and say with glee:
"What caused my death you'll never know—
   Perhaps my mother murdered me."

When I went into court again,
   To hear the mother's evidence—
It was a love-child, she explained.
   And smiled, for our intelligence.

"Now, Gentlemen of the Jury," said
   The coroner—"this woman's child
By misadventure met its death."
   "Aye, aye," said we. The mother smiled.

And I could see that child's one eye
   Which seemed to laugh, and say with glee:
"What caused my death you'll never know—
   Perhaps my mother murdered me."

THE BUST

When I went wandering far from home,
I left a woman in my room
To clean my hearth and floor, and dust
My shelves and pictures, books and bust.

When I came back a welcome glow
Burned in her eyes—her voice was low;
And every thing was in its place,
As clean and bright as her own face.

But when I looked more closely there,
The dust was on my dark, bronze hair;
The nose and eyebrows too were white—
And yet the lips were clean and bright.

The years have gone, and so has she,
But still the truth remains with me—
How that hard mouth was once kept clean
By living lips that kissed unseen.

W. H. Davies lived much of his life in poverty, and in sickening surroundings. It never made him angry, at least not in his poems. But out of the mining valleys of South Wales, there were poets who were beginning to write in a spirit of passionate anger against the inequality of social conditions. They wrote, not of the truths and beauties of the natural world, but of the lies and ugliness of the unnatural system of society under which they worked—or, more often during the nineteen-twenties and thirties, under which they were not allowed to work. They spoke, in ragged and angry rhythms, of the Wales *they* knew: the coaltips, the dole-queues, the stubborn bankrupt villages, the children, scrutting for coal on the slagheaps, the colliers' shabby allotments, the cheapjack cinema, the whippet races, the disused quarries, the still pit-wheels, the gaunt tin-roofed chapels in the soot, the hewers squatting in the cut, the pubs, the Woolworths, the deacons and the gyppos, silicosis, little Moscow up beyond the hills, sag-roof factory and plumeless stack, stone-grey street, scummed river, the capped and mufflered knots of men outside the grim Employment Exchange and the Public Library. Among these poets, Idris Davies is perhaps the only one who has attempted to shape his violence into real poems, and he often achieves a lyrical simplicity which in no way lessens the intensity of his hatred of injustice. In some of his poems he can even bring himself to write with a kind of sad and jaunty happiness about his people and his country, as in:—

THE ANGRY SUMMER

He won't talk any more of the distant days
Of his childhood in the coalface and the tavern
And all his cronies who had left him behind
In the ragged little hut by the river;
He who had given so much of his sweat
In the days of his youth and his vigour,
Now falling like a wrinkled apple into a ditch
To rot away in the everlasting dust of death.
Tonight he shall sleep in a grave on the slope,
And no more will he prattle of the days of his youth.

WELSH POETS   69

Days of the Truck System and the Tory Sabbath,
And the Chartists and the starved-out strikers.
No more will he lean on the bridge in the summer morning
And make a god of Gladstone and a devil of Disraeli,
And go into raptures on the young Lloyd George
Who strode into London with a dazzling sword,
A bright St. David from the stormy mountain.
All his long and luckless days are over,
And the broken old body in the plain deal coffin
Will be deaf to all the birds above the hill,
The larks that sing and sing in the cloudless sky
As the men move away in slow black clusters
Down on the road to the colliery town.

And Idris Davies has written, too, in *Gwalia Deserta,*
one very simple and moving song:—

> O what can you give me?
> Say the sad bells of Rhymney.
>
> Is there hope for the future?
> Cry the brown bells of Merthyr.
>
> Who made the mineowner?
> Say the black bells of Rhondda.
>
> And who robbed the miner?
> Cry the grim bells of Blaina.
>
> They will plunder willy-nilly,
> Say the bells of Caerphilly.
>
> They have fangs, they have teeth,
> Shout the loud bells of Neath.
>
> The south, things are sullen,
> Say the pink bells of Brecon.
>
> Even God is uneasy,
> Say the moist bells of Swansea.

Put the vandals in court!
Cry the bells of Newport.

All would be well if—if—if—
Say the green bells of Cardiff.

Why so worried, sisters, why?
Sing the silver bells of Wye.

GLYN JONES

Glyn Jones, now a schoolmaster, is one of the few young
Welshmen writing English poetry today who has a deep knowledge of *Welsh* poetry itself, and he has tried, in several English
poems, to use the very difficult ancient bardic forms. These forms
rely on a great deal of assonance and alliteration and most com-
plicated internal rhyming; and these effects in English have, in
the hands of the few who have attempted to use them, succeeded
only in warping, crabbing and obscuring the natural genius of
the English language. But, when Glyn Jones is not experimenting
in what must always be, to ears accustomed to English poetry,
unavoidably awkward sound and syntax, he can write as surely
as this. The poem, in which I think you will be able to detect,
straight away, the influence of D. H. Lawrence, especially in the
last stanza, is called:—

ESYLLT

As he climbs down our hill, my kestrel rises,
Steering in silence up from five empty fields,
A smooth sun brushed brown across his shoulders,
Floating in wide circles, his warm wings stiff.
Their shadows cut; in new soft orange hunting boots
My lover crashes through the snapping bracken.

The still gorse-hissing hill burns, brags gold broom's
Outcropping quartz; each touched bush spills dew.
Strangely last moment's parting was never sad,
But unreal like my promised years; less felt
Than this intense white silver snail calligraphy
Scrawled here in the sun across these stones.

Why have I often wanted to cry out
More against his going when he has left my flesh
Only for the night? When he has gone out
Hot from my mother's kitchen, and my combs
Were on the table under the lamp, and the wind
Was banging the doors of the shed in the yard.

ALUN LEWIS

And so, lastly, we come to Alun Lewis, who was killed by
accident, while serving in India, in 1944. Three of the very
finest—perhaps *the* very finest it will be found, in another and
a quieter day—of the poets who wrote in the two Great Wars
of this century were Edward Thomas, Wilfred Owen, and Alun
Lewis. All three were Welshmen. I have no comment, of any
national reference, to add to that. Lewis was a healer and an
illuminator, humble before his own confessions, awed before the
eternal confession of love by the despised and condemned inhabitants of the world crumbling around him. He wrote:

I have no more desire to express
The old relationships, of love fulfilled
Or stultified, capacity for pain,
Nor to say gracefully all that the poets have said
Of one or other of the old compulsions.
For now the times are gathered for confession.

And always humbly, never as a priest but as a servant, he heard
them. He knew, like Wilfred Owen, that, in war, the poetry is in
the pity. And, like Owen, he could never place himself above pity
but must give it tongue. Here is an extract from an unfinished
play in which Sacco, the comrade of Vanzetti, writes from prison
to his son:

And for yourself, remember in the play
Of happiness you must not act alone.
The joy is in the sharing of the feast.
Also be like a man in how you greet
The suffering that makes your young face thin.
Be not perturbed if you are called to fight.
Only a fool thinks life was made his way,
A fool or the daughter of a wealthy house.

Alun Lewis was young to have the courage of his faith to say this. Listen to these verses from "Odi et Amo":

> Yet in this blood-soaked forest of disease
> Where wolfish men lie scorched and black
> And corpses sag against the trees
> And love's dark roots writhe back
>
> Like snakes into the scorching earth;
> In this corrupted wood where none can hear
> The love songs of Ophelia
> And the laughter of Lear,
>
> My soul cries out with love
> Of all that walk and swim and fly.
> From the mountains, from the sky,
> Out of the depths of the sea
> Love cries and cries in me
>
> And summer blossoms break above my head
> With all the unbearable beauty of the dead.

And this poem, "Christmas Holiday":—

> Big-uddered piebald cattle low
> The shivering chestnut stallion dozes
> The fat wife sighs in her chair
> Her lap is filled with paper roses
> The poacher sleeps in the goose-girl's arms
> Incurious after so much eating
> All human beings are replete.
>
> But the cock upon the dunghill feels
> God's needle quiver in his brain
> And thrice he crows: and at the sound
> The sober and the tipsy men
> Jump out of bed with one accord
> And start the war again.
> The fat wife comfortably sleeping
> Sighs and licks her lips and smiles
>
> But the goose-girl is weeping.

And, last of all, "The Sentry":—

> I have begun to die
> For now at last I know
> That there is no escape
> From Night. Not any dream
> Nor breathless images of sleep
> Touch my bat's-eyes. I hang
> Leathery-arid from the hidden roof
> Of Night, and sleeplessly
> I watch within Sleep's province.
> I have left
> The lovely bodies of the boy and girl
> Deep in each other's placid arms;
> And I have left
> The beautiful lanes of sleep
> That barefoot lovers follow to this last
> Cold shore of thought I guard.
> I have begun to die
> And the guns' implacable silence
> Is my black interim, my youth and age,
> In the flower of fury, the folded poppy,
> Night.

(1946)

WILFRED OWEN

"This book is not about heroes. English Poetry is not yet fit to speak of them.

"Nor is it about deeds, or lands, nor anything about glory, honour, might, majesty, dominion, or power, except War.

"Above all I am not concerned with Poetry.

"My subject is War and the pity of War.

"The Poetry is in the pity.

"Yet these elegies are to this generation in no sense consolatory. They may be to the next. All a poet can do today is warn. That is why the true Poets must be truthful."

And that is the Preface, by Wilfred Owen, to a volume of his poems which was to show, to England, and the intolerant world, the foolishness, unnaturalness, horror, inhumanity, and insupportability of War, and to expose, so that all could suffer and see, the heroic lies, the willingness of the old to sacrifice the young, indifference, grief, the Souls of Soldiers.

The volume, as Wilfred Owen visualised it in trench and shell hole and hospital, in the lunatic centre of battle, in the collapsed and apprehensive calm of sick-leave, never appeared. But many of the poems that were to have been included in the volume remain, their anguish unabated, their beauty for ever, their truth manifest, their warning unheeded.

Wilfred Owen was born in 1893 and killed in 1918. Twenty-five years of age, he was the greatest poet of the first Great War. Perhaps, in the future, if there are men, then, still to read—by which I mean, if there are men at all—he may be regarded as one of the great poets of all wars. But only War itself can resolve the problem of the ultimate truth of his, or of anyone else's poetry: War, or its cessation.

And this time, when, in the words of an American critic, the audiences of the earth, witnessing what well may be the last act of their own tragedy, insist upon chief actors who are senseless enough to perform a cataclysm, the voice of the poetry of Wilfred Owen speaks to us, down the revolving stages of thirty years, with terrible new significance and strength. We had not forgotten his poetry, but perhaps we had allowed ourselves to think of it as the voice of one particular time, one place, one war. Now, at the beginning of what, in the future, may never be known to historians as the "atomic age"—for obvious reasons: there may be no historians—we can see, rereading Owen, that he is a poet of all times, all places, and all wars. There is only one War: that of men against men.

Owen left to us less than sixty poems, many of them complete works of art, some of them fragments, some of them in several versions of revision, the last poem of them all dying away in the middle of a line: "Let us sleep now. . . ." I shall not try to follow his short life, from the first imitations of his beloved Keats to the last prodigious whisper of "sleep" down the profound and echoing tunnels of "Strange Meeting." Mr. Edmund Blunden, in the introduction to his probably definitive edition of the poems, has done that with skill and love. His collected poems make a little, huge book, working—and always he worked on his poems like fury, or a poet—from a lush ornamentation of language, brilliantly, borrowed melody, and ingenuous sentiment, to dark, grave, assonant rhythms, vocabulary purged and sinewed, wrathful pity and prophetic utterance.

But these are all words, my words. Let us hear him, before we try to see him, in some kind of flame-lit perspective, on the battlefields of France and the earth. This poem is called:

EXPOSURE

Our brains ache, in the merciless iced east winds that knive us . . .
Wearied we keep awake because the night is silent . . .
Low, drooping flares confuse our memory of the salient . . .
Worried by silence, sentries whisper, curious, nervous,
        But nothing happens.

Watching, we hear the mad gusts tugging on the wire,
Like twitching agonies of men among its brambles.
Northward, incessantly, the flickering gunnery rumbles,
Far off, like a dull rumour of some other war.
        What are we doing here?

The poignant misery of dawn begins to grow . . .
We only know war lasts, rain soaks, and clouds sag stormy.
Dawn massing in the east her melancholy army
Attacks once more in ranks on shivering ranks of gray,
        But nothing happens.

Sudden successive flights of bullets streak the silence.
Less deadly than the air that shudders black with snow,
With sidelong flowing flakes that flock, pause, and renew,
We watch them wandering up and down the wind's nonchalance,
        But nothing happens.

Pale flakes with fingering stealth come feeling for our faces—
We cringe in holes, back on forgotten dreams, and stare, snow-
    dazed,
Deep into grassier ditches. So we drowse, sun-dozed,
Littered with blossoms trickling where the blackbird fusses.
        Is it that we are dying?

Slowly our ghosts drag home: glimpsing the sunk fires, glozed
With crusted dark-red jewels; crickets jingle there;
For hours the innocent mice rejoice: the house is theirs;
Shutters and doors, all closed: on us the doors are closed,—
        We turn back to our dying.

Since we believe not otherwise can kind fires burn;
Nor ever suns smile true on child, or field, or fruit.
For God's invincible spring our love is made afraid;
Therefore, not loath, we lie out here; therefore were born,
        For love of God seems dying.

To-night, His frost will fasten on this mud and us,
Shrivelling many hands, puckering foreheads crisp.
The burying-party, picks and shovels in their shaking grasp,
Pause over half-known faces. All their eyes are ice,
        But nothing happens.

    Who wrote this? A boy of twenty-three or four, comfortably
born and educated, serious, "literary," shy, never "exposed" before to anything harsher than a Channel crossing, fond of *En-*

dymion and the open air, fresh from a tutor's job. Earlier, in letters to his mother, he had written from the Somme, in 1917, in that infernal winter: "There is a fine heroic feeling about being in France, and I am in perfect spirits. . . ." Or again, he talked of his companions: "The roughest set of knaves I have ever been herded with." When he heard the guns for the first time, he said: "It was a sound not without a certain sublimity."

It was *this* young man, at first reacting so conventionally to his preconceived ideas of the "glory of battle"—and such ideas he was to slash and scorify a very short time afterwards—who wrote the poem? It was this young man, steel-helmeted, buff-jerkined, gauntleted, rubber-waded, in the freezing rain of the flooded trenches, in the mud that was not mud but an octopus of sucking clay, who wrote:

ANTHEM FOR DOOMED YOUTH

What passing-bells for these who die as cattle?
   Only the monstrous anger of the guns.
   Only the stuttering rifles' rapid rattle
Can patter out their hasty orisons.
No mockeries for them from prayers or bells,
   Nor any voice of mourning save the choirs,—
The shrill, demented choirs of wailing shells;
   And bugles calling for them from sad shires.

What candles may be held to speed them all?
   Not in the hands of boys, but in their eyes
Shall shine the holy glimmers of good-byes.
   The pallor of girls' brows shall be their pall;
Their flowers the tenderness of silent minds,
And each slow dusk a drawing-down of blinds.

There is no contradiction here. The studious, healthy young man with a love of poetry, as we see him set against the safe background of school, university, and tutordom, is precisely the same as the sombre but radiant, selfless, decrying and exalting, infinitely tender, humble, harrowed seer and stater of the "Anthem for Doomed Youth" and for himself. There is no difference. Only, the world has happened to him. And everything, as Yeats once said, happens in a blaze of light.

The world had happened to him. All its suffering moved about and within him. And his intense pity for all human fear, pain, and grief was given trumpet-tongue. He knew, as surely as though the words had been spoken to him aloud, as indeed they had been though they were the words of wounds, the shape of the dead, the colour of blood, he knew he stood alone among men to *plead* for them in their agony, to blast the walls of ignorance, pride, pulpit and state. He stood like Everyman, in No Man's Land: "It is like the eternal place of gnashing of teeth; the Slough of Despond could be contained in one of its crater-holes; the fires of Sodom and Gomorrah could not light a candle to it—to find the way to *Babylon the Fallen*." And out of this, he wrote the poem called:

GREATER LOVE

Red lips are not so red
   As the stained stones kissed by the English dead.
Kindness of wooed and wooer
Seems shame to their love pure.
O Love, your eyes lose lure
   When I behold eyes blinded in my stead!

Your slender attitude
   Trembles not exquisite like limbs knife-skewed,
Rolling and rolling there
Where God seems not to care;
Till the fierce Love they bear
   Cramps them in death's extreme decrepitude.

Your voice sings not so soft,—
   Though even as wind murmuring through raftered loft,—
Your dear voice is not dear,
Gentle, and evening clear,
As theirs whom none now hear,
   Now earth has stopped their piteous mouths that coughed.

WILFRED OWEN   79

Heart, you were never hot,
  Nor large, nor full like hearts made great with shot;
And though your hand be pale,
Paler are all which trail
Your cross through flame and hail:
  Weep, you may weep, for you may touch them not.

It was impossible for him to avoid the sharing of suffering.
He could not record a wound that was not his own. He had so
very many deaths to die, and so very short a life within which to
endure them all. It's no use trying to imagine what would have
happened to Owen had he lived on. Owen, at twenty-six or so,
exposed to the hysteria and exploded values of false peace. Owen
alive now, at the age of fifty-three, and half the world starving.
You cannot generalize about age and poetry. A man's poems, if
they are good poems, are always older than himself; and sometimes they are ageless. We know that the shape and the texture of
his poems would always be restlessly changing, though the purpose behind them would surely remain unalterable; he would
always be experimenting technically, deeper and deeper driving
towards the final intensity of language: the words behind words.
Poetry is, of its nature, an experiment. All poetical impulses are
towards the creation of adventure. And adventure is movement.
And the end of each adventure is a new impulse to move again
towards creation. Owen, had he lived, would never have ceased
experiment; and so powerful was the impetus behind his work,
and so intricately strange his always growing mastery of words,
he would never have ceased to influence the work of his contemporaries. Had he lived, English poetry would not be the same.
The course of poetry is dictated by accidents. Even so, he is one
of the four most profound influences upon the poets who came
after him; the other three being Gerard Manley Hopkins, the
later W. B. Yeats, and T. S. Eliot.

But we must go back, from our guesses and generalisations
and abstractions, to Owen's poetry itself; to the brief, brave life
and the enduring words. In hospital, labelled as a "neurasthenic
case," he observed, and experienced, the torments of the living
dead, and he has expressed their "philosophy" in the dreadful
poem—

À TERRE

(Being the philosophy of many soldiers)

Sit on the bed. I'm blind, and three parts shell.
Be careful; can't shake hands now; never shall.
Both arms have mutinied against me,—brutes.
My fingers fidget like ten idle brats.

I tried to peg out soldierly,—no use!
One dies of war like any old disease.
This bandage feels like pennies on my eyes.
I have my medals?—Discs to make eyes close.
My glorious ribbons?——Ripped from my own back
In scarlet shreds. (That's for your poetry book.)

A short life and a merry one, my buck!
We used to say we'd hate to live dead-old,—
Yet now . . . I'd willingly be puffy, bald,
And patriotic. Buffers catch from boys
At least the jokes hurled at them. I suppose
Little I'd ever teach a son, but hitting,
Shooting, war, hunting, all the arts of hurting.
Well, that's what I learnt,—that, and making money.

Your fifty years ahead seem none too many?
Tell me how long I've got? God! For one year
To help myself to nothing more than air!
One Spring! Is one too good to spare, too long?
Spring wind would work its own way to my lung,
And grow me legs as quick as lilac-shoots.

My servant's lamed, but listen how he shouts!
When I'm lugged out, he'll still be good for that.
Here in this mummy-case, you know, I've thought
How well I might have swept his floors for ever.
I'd ask no nights off when the bustle's over,
Enjoying so the dirt. Who's prejudiced
Against a grimed hand when his own's quite dust,
Less live than specks that in the sun-shafts turn,

Less warm than dust that mixes with arms' tan?
I'd love to be a sweep, now, black as Town,
Yes; or a muckman. Must I be his load?

O Life, Life, let me breathe,—a dug-out rat!
Not worse than ours the existences rats lead—
Nosing along at night down some safe rut,
They find a shell-proof home before they rot.
Dead men may envy living mites in cheese,
Or good germs even. Microbes have their joys,
And subdivide, and never come to death.
Certainly flowers have the easiest time on earth.
"I shall be one with nature, herb, and stone,"
Shelley would tell me. Shelley would be stunned:
The dullest Tommy hugs that fancy now.
"Pushing up daisies" is their creed, you know.
To grain, then, go my fat, to buds my sap,
For all the usefulness there is in soap.
D'you think the Boche will ever stew man-soup?
Some day, no doubt, if . . .
                              Friend, be very sure
I shall be better off with plants that share
More peaceably the meadow and the shower.
Soft rains will touch me,—as they could touch once,
And nothing but the sun shall make me ware.
Your guns may crash around me. I'll not hear;
Or, if I wince, I shall not know I wince.
Don't take my soul's poor comfort for your jest.
Soldiers may grow a soul when turned to fronds,
But here the thing's best left at home with friends.

My soul's a little grief, grappling your chest,
To climb your throat on sobs; easily chased
On other sighs and wiped by fresher winds.

Carry my crying spirit till it's weaned
To do without what blood remained these wounds.

To see him in his flame-lit perspective, against the background now of the poxed and cratered warscape, shivering in the

snow under the slitting wind, marooned on a frozen desert, or crying, in a little oven of mud, that his "senses are charred," is to see a man consigned to articulate immolation. He buries his smashed head with his own singed hands, and is himself the intoning priest over the ceremony, the suicide, the sunset. He is the common touch. He is the bell of the church of the broken body. He writes love letters home for the illiterate dead. Ignorant, uncaring, hapless as the rest of the bloody troops, he is their arguer shell-shocked into diction, though none may understand. He is content to be the unhonoured prophet in death's country: for fame, as he said, was the last infirmity he desired.

None of the poems you have heard were published while Owen was alive; indeed, he saw little or nothing of his in print. But I don't want to give the impression that he wrote always in intellectual loneliness, or that he carried his poems about with him like dark, incommunicable secrets. Siegfried Sassoon has described how, when he was in a nursing home for what were then called "shell-shock cases," Owen, a stranger, came into his room with a number of Sassoon's newly published book of poems, and, shyly, asked him if he would autograph them. And Sassoon and Owen talked about poetry, Sassoon, as he himself said, rather laying down the law to this unassuming, shy young man. And Owen, on leaving, gave him some poems and asked him if he'd have a look at them and tell him if they were any good. And Sassoon saw that they were good. And so did several other poets and men of letters to whom Sassoon sent them. And arrangements were made for a book of them to be published. Owen never saw that book.

There are many aspects of Owen's life and work upon which I haven't touched at all. I have laboured, in these notes or pieces between poems, only one argument, and that inherent in the poems themselves. Owen's words have shown, for me, and I hope (and know) for you, the position-in-calamity which, without intellectual choice, he chose to take. But remember, he was not a "wise man" in the sense that he had achieved, for himself, a true way of believing. He believed there was no one true way because all ways are by-tracked and rutted and pitfalled with ignorance and injustice and indifference. He was himself diffident and self-distrustful. He had to be wrong, clumsy, affected often, ambiguous, bewildered. Like every man at last, he had to fight the whole war by himself. He lost, and he won. In a letter written towards the end of his life and many deaths, he quoted from Rabindranath Tagore: "When I go hence, let this be my parting word, that what I have seen is unsurpassable."

He was killed on November 4, 1918. This is his last, and unfinished poem, found among his papers, after his death.

STRANGE MEETING

It seemed that out of battle I escaped
Down some profound dull tunnel, long since scooped
Through granites which titanic wars had groined.
Yet also there encumbered sleepers groaned,
Too fast in thought or death to be bestirred.
Then, as I probed them, one sprang up, and stared
With piteous recognition in fixed eyes,
Lifting distressful hands as if to bless.
And by his smile, I knew that sullen hall,
By his dead smile I knew we stood in Hell.
With a thousand pains that vision's face was grained;
Yet no blood reached there from the upper ground,
And no guns thumped, or down the flues made moan.
"Strange friend," I said, "here is no cause to mourn."
"None," said the other, "save the undone years,
The hopelessness. Whatever hope is yours,
Was my life also; I went hunting wild
After the wildest beauty in the world,
Which lies not calm in eyes, or braided hair,
But mocks the steady running of the hour,
And if it grieves, grieves richlier than here.
For by my glee might many men have laughed,
And of my weeping something had been left,
Which must die now. I mean the truth untold,
The pity of war, the pity war distilled.
Now men will go content with what we spoiled.
Or, discontent, boil bloody, and be spilled.
They will be swift with swiftness of the tigress,
None will break ranks, though nations trek from progress.
Courage was mine, and I had mystery,
Wisdom was mine, and I had mastery;

To miss the march of this retreating world
Into vain citadels that are not walled.
Then, when much blood had clogged their chariot-wheels
I would go up and wash them from sweet wells,
Even with truths that lie too deep for taint.
I would have poured my spirit without stint
But not through wounds; not on the cess of war.
Foreheads of men have bled where no wounds were.
I am the enemy you killed, my friend.
I knew you in this dark; for so you frowned
Yesterday through me as you jabbed and killed.
I parried; but my hands were loath and cold.
Let us sleep now. . . ."

(1946)

SIR PHILIP SIDNEY

It is among the arguments of the *Defence of Poesie* that the Poet is the greatest teacher of knowledge because he teaches by a divine delightfulness. "For," wrote Sir Philip Sidney, "he doth not only show the way, but giveth so sweet a prospect into the way, as will entice any man to enter into it: Nay he doth as if your journey should lie through a fair vineyard, at the verie first, give you a cluster of grapes, that full of that taste, you may long to pass further. He beginneth not with obscure definitions, which must blur the margent with interpretations, and load the memory with doubtfulness: but he cometh to you with words set in delightful proportion, either accompanied with, or prepared for the well enchanting skill of *Music,* and with a tale forsooth he cometh unto you, with a tale, which holdeth children from play, and old men from the chimney corner."

The *Defense of Poesie* is a defence of the imaginative life, of the duty, and the delight, of the individual poet living among men in the middle of the turning world that has, in his time, so little time for him. Sometimes melancholy, often distant, proud and politic, delicate and hotheaded, unperturbedly honest, he exercised a grave fascination upon all who met him. He deliberated upon himself with gravity, and found it delightful or distasteful as the wind of love blew, as the life of Elizabeth's court grew perilous, lax, fickle, or degraded, as shallow justice shook, as adventurers sailed with wrong maps round the real rich roaring globe.

Even when he was a child at Penshurst or in Wales, his parents, seeing him such a grave boy, "adjured him to be merry." He was praised, while a child, by Fulke Greville, for being of "such staidness of mind, lovely and familiar gravity, as carried grace and reverence above greater years."

Sir Philip Sidney's mother was the daughter of John Dudley, the Duke of Northumberland who was beheaded for his part in the placing of Lady Jane Grey upon the throne of England. That little reign brought death and desolation to all his mother's kin. Sidney could never have forgotten what his mother must have told him: Lady Mary Sidney who nursed Queen Elizabeth through smallpox and who caught the disease herself so horribly that, even at home, she always wore a mask; he never could have forgotten that Guildford Dudley, his mother's brother, married Jane Grey; that on her way to be made queen, dressed in green velvet, she was so slight and small she was mounted on a very high chopines to make her look taller. "She was 16, Guilford was a very tall strong boy with light hair, who paid her much attention." On her way to the scaffold she carried a prayer book, and wore black.

Sidney's father, Sir Henry, was the ablest governor of Ireland under Elizabeth. He wrote to his very young son, then a scholar at Shrewsbury school, this mature advice:

"Seldom drink wine, and yet sometimes do, lest being enforced to drink upon the sudden you should find yourself inflamed.

"Be courteous of gesture and affable to all men, with diversity of reverences according to the dignity of the person: there is nothing that winneth so much for so little cost.

"Give yourself to be merry, for you degenerate from your father if you find not yourself most able in wit and body and to do anything when you be most merry: but let your mirth be ever void of all scurrility and biting words to any man."

Three important events, of the little that is known, occurred in Sidney's boyhood:

He and Fulke Greville, who was afterwards to write so much and so movingly about him, entered Shrewsbury on the same day, in 1564.

In 1566, when he was twelve, he was presented with the poems of Virgil. And in the summer of that year he was summoned by his uncle, the Earl of Leicester and Chancellor of the University, to go from Shrewsbury to Oxford, where he saw, for the first time, Queen Elizabeth in her, to his young eyes, uncomplicated glory.

Sidney, as a child, was of a charming and ingenuous appearance, as Thomas Moffett, in his recently discovered and translated *Nobilis and Lessus Lugubris,* testifies:

He was "endowed with gifts of nature, with a strong and

almost manly voice, and, in fine, with a certain consistent and
absolute perfection of mind and body. . . . When as a three-year-
old he beheld the moon, with clean hands and head covered he
used to pray to it and devoutly to worship. . . ." Here follows
Sidney's sonnet:

WITH HOW SAD STEPS, ô MOONE

With how sad steps, ô Moone, thou climb'st the skies,
    How silently, and with how wanne a face,
    What may it be, that even in heav'nly place
    That busie archer his sharpe arrowes tries?

Sure if that long with *Love* acquainted eyes
    Can judge of *Love,* thou feel'st a Lovers case;
    I reade it in thy lookes, thy languisht grace
    To me that feele the like, thy state descries.

Then ev'n of fellowship, ô Moone, tell me,
    Is constant *Love* deem'd there but want of wit?
    Are Beauties there as proud as here they be?

Do they above love to be lov'd, and yet
    Those Lovers scorne whom that *Love* doth possesse?
    Do they call *Vertue* there ungratefulnesse?

The Earl of Leicester, then favoured by the Queen, made
sure that his nephew was a pretty boy to see her, bought him
damask gowns trimmed with velvet, doublets of crimson and green
taffeta, jerkins of blue leather, hose of carnation, shoes of white
and green and blue. And he saw Elizabeth come into Oxford,
clothed in scarlet silk and gold, with headdress of spun gold,
her mantle of purple and ermine, and according to some historians, she sat on a high gold seat in an open litter drawn by
mules.

In 1572, when he was eighteen, he received the Queen's
license to undertake a two years' visit to the Continent.

Attached to the suite of the Earl of Lincoln, he went first
to Paris: "a grave and tender handsome youth," or, as his uncle
Leicester wrote in a letter to Walsingham, Ambassador to France,
"young and raw." A convinced and zealous Protestant by birth,
education, and inclination, he was present at the anarchic eve of

St. Bartholomew's Day when an unknown number of thousands of Protestants perished. At Frankfurt, he stayed at the shop of the scholarly printer, Andrew Wechel, where he met the learned Protestant controversialist, Hubert Languet, to whom, he confessed, he owed all his knowledge of literature and true religion. He visited Strasbourg, Vienna, Venice, Genoa, Florence, Padua (where he studied astronomy, geometry, music and Greek); he travelled to Poland and came home.

Leicester at once placed him at court, at Greenwich, where Elizabeth at the age of forty-two was, as Sidney wrote, "somewhat advanced in years." He was taught to be a courtier. He was at Kenilworth, in the dazzling, rippling, musical summer of 1575, where there were unforgettable pageants for the Queen, masques and fireworks, the playing of gittern and cithern and virginals, tilts and jousts, bearbaiting, morris-dancing, tournaments, water-plays, and drinking from great livery pots of silver filled with claret and white wine.

In 1576, with the Earl of Essex, he joined his father in Ireland, and fought the boggish and cantankerous Irish who did not think, as he did, that English law was, in all the world, the most just and agreeable.

There Essex died, leaving a message for Sidney: "Tell him I aned him nothing, but I wish him well, and so well that if God do move their hearts, I wish that he might match with my daughter. I call him son; he is so wise, so virtuous, and so godly; and if he go on in the course he hath begun, he will be as famous and worthy a gentleman as ever England bred."

The daughter of Essex was Penelope Devereux, the "Stella" of the sonnets. Court life, home in England, proved expensive and lowering. His subsequent ambassadorship to the imperial court of Austria was splendid and unimportant. What he wanted, above all, was to serve the cause of Protestant religion. The Queen allowed him no opportunities. His uncle Leicester was disgraced, almost fatally, by the Queen's discovery of his hidden marriage. The Queen herself was about to contract an unfortunate marriage with the house of Anjou. Sidney wrote to her his charming Discourse to the Queen's Majesty touching upon the affair and graciously attempting to dissuade her from it; for which he received no thanks. He challenged the unpleasant Earl of Oxford to a duel. John Stubbes, who had written a pamphlet expressing the feelings of the common people against Elizabeth's proposed marriage, had his offending right hand cut off with mallet and butcher's cleaver. And Sidney was, fortunately, so depressed by life in London, that he retired, from unemployment at court, to the company of his sister, the Countess of Pembroke, at Wilton House, in the Hundred of Branch and Dale, Wiltshire, there to write his *Arcadia*.

Wilton was begun in the time of Henry VIII, under the conduct of Hans Holbein, and finished in the time of Edward VI for the first Earl of Pembroke. The garden of Wilton that Sir Philip Sidney knew and loved can be seen in an old print. Here are the embroydered plots with their four fountaynes; the plots of flowers, and beyond them the little terras. Here are groves through which passes the river Nader, and statues of Bacchus and Flora, and covered arbors, and great ponds with fountains and columns and two crownes spinning on the top of the water; and a compartiment of greens, and cherry trees; and the great oval with the brass Gladiator; more arbors and turning gallaryes, porticos, and a terrace whose steps are sea-monsters.

Here was the most perfect house and garden for the writing of an Arcadian romance thronged with enchantments and disguised princes, murders, shepherds, sports, potions, and many kinds of love.

This enormously involved story, written in prose, and interspersed with songs and eclogues in verse, is dedicated "To My Dear Lady and Sister, the Countess of Pembroke."

"Here now have you (most dear, and most worthy to be the most dear Lady) this idle work of mine, which, I fear (like the spider's webbe) will be thought fitter to be swept away than worn to any other purpose."

But here was no filigree web of words, but a huge tapestry woven to bewilder and to keep out the light. It is all ornament, spectacle and splendour, pageantry, pomp, and sumptuous profusion, frill, lace, gold and jewel, paradox, jingle, personification, descriptions of natural scenery and ethical reflections, battles, tournaments, sad shepherd's sheepish lyrics, all blurring beautifully and drowning at triumphal length.

He had written poetical theory, and now he tried his hand at poetical experiment, "freely ranging within the Zodiack of his owne wit."

The garlands hang their all to windy heads; the colours run and vanish; the cornucopia is full of holes; rhymes hang blowsy on the brow of the melting monument. How few the clear calm seconds in that rich desert of stationary time: these lines, perhaps, or are they too "dainty"?

"The messenger made speed, and found Argalus at a castle of his own, sitting in a parlour with the fair Parthenia, he reading in a book the stories of Hercules, she by him, as to hear him read; but while his eyes looked on the book she looked on his eyes, and sometimes staying him with some pretty question, not so much to be resolved of the doubt as to give him occasion to look upon her. A happy couple he joying in her, she joying in herself, but in herself because she enjoyed him."

And the famous description of the water-spaniel. And the eminently malicious line, interpreted by some critics as a statement of chivalrous loyalty: "She was a queen, and therefore beautiful."

But it is only in the sonnet sequence, *Astrophel and Stella,* that he is to be seen as a great poet. It was published five years after his death, in 1591. Nash says of it: "This tragic-comedy of love is performed by starlight."

The sonnets are addressed to Penelope Devereux, whose father wished Sidney to marry her. They begin with elegance and pretence, poems moving like courtiers dressed in the habit of love. They are *about* love, they are not *in* love; they *address* love, they do not speak *out* of it. The raptures are almost easily come by; the despair almost as easily relinquished. They are the most perfect exercises for a man about to be in love. And Penelope married, and Sidney had lost her, and the sonnets were no longer rehearsals for a poetic event but poetry itself, striding and burning:

> I might, unhappy word, (woe me) I might,
> And then would not, nor could not see my blisse:
> Tyll now, wrapt in a most infernall Night,
> I finde, how heavenly day (wretch) did I misse;
> Hart rent thy selfe, thou doost thy selfe but right,
>   No lovely *Paris* made thy *Helen* his,
>   No force, no fraude, rob'd thee of thy delight,

No Fortune of thy fortune Author is;
But to my selfe, my selfe did give the blow,
While too much wit forsooth so troubled me,
That I respects for both our sakes must showe.
And could I not by rysing morne fore-see,
How faire a day was neere, (ô punisht eyes)
That I had beene more foolish, or more wise.

In these sonnets we see, held still in time for us, a whole
progress of passion, physical and spiritual, coursing through rage
and despair, self-pity, hope renewed, exultancy, moon-moved
dreams, black fear and blinding bright certainty of final loss.

There are several songs among the sonnets. In the eighth
song, Stella gently kills his hope of possessing her.

In a grove most rich of shade;
Where birds wanton Musicke made:
Maie then young his pide weeds shewing,
New perfumes with flowers fresh growing.

In the storming of Zutphen in the Netherlands, September
22, 1586, Sir Philip Sidney was struck by a musket-ball in the
thigh. On his agonized way back to the camp, "being thirsty with
excess of bleeding, he called for drink, which was presently
brought him; but, as he was putting the bottle to his mouth, he
saw a poor soldier carried along, who had eaten his last at the
same feast, ghastly casting up his eyes at the bottle, which Sir
Philip, perceiving, took it from his head before he drank, and
delivered it to the poor man with these words, 'Thy necessity is
yet greater than mine.'"

The operations upon his wound were long and painful.
"When they began to dress his wound, he, both by way of charge
and advice, told them that while his strength was still entire, his
body free from fever, and his mind able to endure, they might
freely use their art, cut, and search to the bottom."

They used their art, and he was taken away to Arnheim.
There he suffered. He became a mere skeleton. The shoulder
bones broke through the skin.

"He one morning lifting up the clothes for change and ease
of his body, smelt some extraordinary noisome savour about him,

differing from oils and salves, as he conceived. . . ." Mortification had set in.

He sent for ministers of many nationalities, and they prayed with him.

He asked for music.

He dictated his will.

He wrote a long letter in Latin.

He bade goodbye to his brother.

Very near death, he said, "I would not change my joy for the empire of the world."

(1947)

ARTISTS OF WALES

Too many of the artists of Wales who go to live permanently in, for example, London, begin almost at once to anglicize themselves beyond recognition—(though this, of course, does not apply to artists alone. I know in London a Welsh hairdresser who has striven so vehemently to abolish his accent that he sounds like a man speaking with the Elgin marbles in his mouth). They ape the narrow "a." They repudiate the Welsh language, whether they know it or not. By the condescending telling of comic apocryphal tales about Dai and Evan from the valleys, they earn, in the company of cultural lickspittles who condescend to them in their turn, sorry dinners and rounds of flat drinks. They fall for the latest isms gullibly as pups for rubber bones. They confirm, by their spaniel adulation and their ignorance of the tradition that inevitably leads to the experiment, the suspicions of un-Welsh experimental artists that all the Welsh are humbugs, especially Welsh artists. In exhibitions, concerts, cocktail parties, there they are on the horn-rimmed edges, stifling their natural ardour so that they may disparagingly drawl, and with knowledgeable satiety, of the paintings, the music, the guests, their host, corseting their voices so that not lilt or inflection of Welsh enthusiasm may exult or pop out. "Ecktually," they say, "I was born in Cwmbwrla, but Soho's better for my gouaches." They set up, in grey, whining London, a little mock Wales of their own, an exile government of dispossessed intellectuals dispossessed not of their country but of their intellects. And they return home, every long now and then, like slummers, airily to treat and backslap their grooved old friends, to enquire, half-laughingly, the whereabouts of streets and buildings as though they did not know them in the deepest dark, to drag, with all the magnets of their snobbery, the Christian names and numbers of wives of aged painters, the haunts of up-and-going poets, the intimate behaviour of the famous musicians whom they have not met, and to jingle in their pockets and mouths their foreign-made pennies, opinions, and intonations.

On the other hand, too many of the artists of Wales stay in Wales too long, giants in the dark behind the parish pump, pygmies in the nationless sun, enviously sniping at the artists of the other countries rather than attempting to raise the standard of art of their own country by working fervently at their own words, paint, or music.

And too many of the artists of Wales spend too much time talking about the position of the artists of Wales.

There is only one position for an artist anywhere: and that is, upright.

(1949)

WALTER DE LA MARE AS A PROSE WRITER

"What I say is, keep on this side of the tomb as long as you can. Don't meddle with that hole. Why? Because while some fine day you will have to go down into it, you can never be quite sure while you are here what mayn't come back out of it.

"There'll be no partings there—I have heard them trolling that out in their chapels like missel-thrushes in the spring. They seem to forget there may be some mighty unpleasant *meetings*. And what about the further shore? It's my belief there's some kind of a ferry plying on that river. And coming back depends on what you want to come back *for*."

So an old, smallish man, muffled in a very respectable great-coat at least two sizes too large for him, mutters in a dark corner of the firelit station waiting-room in Walter de la Mare's uneasy story, "Crewe."

How many of the nasty ghosts, from the other side of the razor's edge, from the wrong room, from the chockablock grave, from the trespassing hereafter, from the sly holes, crawl over and into the seedy waiting-rooms, the creeping railway carriages, the gas-lamped late Victorian teashops the colour of stewed tea, where down-at-soul strangers contrive their tales and, drop by drop, leak out the shadows of their grey or black, forlorn, and vaguely infernal secrets. The ghosts of Mr. de la Mare, though they reek and scamper, and, in old houses at the proper bad hours, are heard sometimes at their infectious business, are not for you to see. But there is no assurance that they do not see you.

And remember, in Mr. de la Mare, the scarecrow that suddently appears in a cornfield behind a house where lately a man has hanged himself. " 'Does the air round the scarecrow strike you as funny at all?' I asked him. 'Out of the way funny—quivering, in a manner of speaking?' 'That's the heat,' he said, but his lip trembled." And the shocking, hallucinatory mask of face and head lying on Mr. Bloom's pillow. And the polluted, invisible presences that seep through the charnel-house of Seton's bloated and grave-emptying Aunt. Here in this house, and in all the other drenched, death-storied houses, down whose corridors and staircases the past hisses, and in whose great mirrors you see behind you a corridor of hinted faces, and in whose lofty beds you share your sheets and nightmare with an intangible, shifted fellow or the sibilant echo of a sound you wish had never been made, most things that happen are ordinary, or very nearly ordinary, and vile. These are houses suspended in time; and timelessness erupts in them.

Mr. de la Mare's *first* world of childhood is as "phantasmal" and "solitary" as Hans Andersen's, but rarely so cruel—or so alive. We grow to know that a huge mythological distance separates that world where Kay and Gerda breathe for ever and that in which the child-alone of de la Mare's tall tales goes about his dreams, loves, and surprises. The country whose habitations, whose great sleepy meadows of March mornings, blue and tumultuous and bleak, faraway cold towers and pinnacles, whether of clouds or hills, valleys and spelled woods, grey-green dells, mistletoed and mustard-seeded avenues, that the children of his earliest stories people, infest, and to high music, moon, glide, and meander through, this is a country of books. Hans Andersen's characters move in a magic that was not, beforehand, composed, pictured, or written down, but is created, there and then, by their lovely motion, and for themselves alone to inhabit. But in, for example, "Henry Brocken," the first of de la Mare's long tales, the world through which the beguiled boy wanders on his mild Rosinanta is made of the trees and climates, moors, mornings and evenings, groves, hills, suns, stars, and gardens, of written, remembered words, of Bunyan's allegory and Swift's satire, of the poetry of Wordsworth, Herrick, Shakespeare, Poe, and Keats. Here enamoured Henry Brocken, in the library country, roving deep in the coils of the necromantic ball, meets Lucy Gray, Jane Eyre, Julia, Electra, Dianame, Anthea, Nick Bottom, the Sleeping Beauty, Gulliver, La Belle Dame Sans Merci, Annabel Lee. But overdecorated, remote, rooted in "reverie," that favourite woollen-headed word, the adventure is all shades. Henry Brocken is a bookish and starry-eyed mood on a borrowed horse. The fabled earth is cloud. Clouds are reflections and echoes of sea waves that rhyme with other words. Rarely just pretty or arch, the way of the story is too often sadly sweet and single-noted.

But as Mr. de la Mare went on writing, his children went on growing. They did not grow into youths, but into children. They lost that lorn and dewy wonder, and when they moved, though always on odd errands, they did not rustle like the pages of an old book turned in a lamplit brown study by a wan, near-tenuous, but inky hand. "Homesick," "forlorn," "lost," and "silent" —these words were used less often, though the nostalgia for the "mournful gaiety" of the past, the loneliness, the silence, and the delirium still were there.

It was through Mr. de la Mare's perception of the very natural oddity and immediacy of childhood that a story like "The Almond Tree" emerged, most movingly, out of the tapestried and *unnatural* "farness" of "Henry Brocken."

Nicholas in "The Almond Tree" is, in Mr. Forrest Reid's words, "the first of a line of strange, wayward, intelligent, dangerously sensitive, infinitely alive small boys." In later stories, his name changes, he is older or younger, sadder or gayer, more darkly cunning or more coldly innocent, now embroiled and tangled in briary thickets of love, now critical and aloof, faintly smiling, in fear and evil occurrences; but always his eyes are the same. It is through these eyes we see the astonishing systems, the unpredictable order, of life on the edge of its answer or quivering on a poisonous threshold.

Only on slight occasions do Mr. de la Mare's children come into contact with each other. We see them, nearly always, in their relation to abnormal men and women. And of his children, it is only the small boys who become real. The little girls live in a distant, and more fragile past.

A *"more* fragile" past; for he is loyal, always, to old Ways and Days, old houses, regions, customs, scents, and colours. His children loiter, wonder, and perceive; his men and women suffer, love, and are haunted; his weathers happen; his dead-behind-the-wainscot blow and scamper, in a time and place that was before he was born. The life of his countryside is that which his mother remembered hearing *her* mother tell of, and of which she told him when he was a child. His imagined memories of childhood are all of a timeless past before his own.

Mr. de la Mare's stories first appeared about 1900. One of the first reviewers to recognise his awakening genius was Francis Thompson. Through all those intermediary years he has written long and short stories, for children, about children, for grown men and dead men, for the unborn, for a livelihood, for nothing, for the best reward, through innocence and with wide and deep skill, for pleasure, for fun, from suffering, and for himself.

His influences? Sir Thomas Browne, de Quincey, Ecclesiastes, Henry James, Emily Brontë, Stevenson, Poe, Traherne. And, in later life, Julian Green perhaps? His style? It is his stories. At the very beginning, he was fond, I think, of a rather flowery verbosity; he used a lot of clichés, but they were always the right ones. There was the suggestion of something, even in a young man, old-maidenish about his attitude to the love of men for women. Country terror was a little cosy, so that you felt not that something nasty had happened in the woodshed but that there were quite hellish goings on among the wool-baskets in the parlour. The period and place about which he writes? Somewhere in rural England, say anywhere after 1830 and just before the afterlife. In his more mature dramatic stories about grown-up human relationships, he often used a convoluted monologue manner that occasionally suggested the ghost of a landbound Conrad talking from behind a pot of ferns. A fault of the prose style, always avoided in the verse, was a gravy-like thickening of texture. And his elaborate language, fuller than ever of artifice and allusion when it was seemingly simple, did not suit, to my mind, the more or less straight-forward, or the grotesque, fairy story. His *real* fairies are as endearing as Dracula. And his subject, always, is the imminence of spiritual danger.

(1946)

A DEARTH OF COMIC WRITERS*

The condition of the world *today* is such that most writers feel they cannot truthfully be "comic" about it. (Was the world ever such that they could?) Perhaps they say: Can we single out the amiably comic eccentricity of individual beings, the ludicrous, the gauche, the maximless gawky, the dear and the daft and the droll, the runcible Booby, the Toby, the Pickwick, the barmy old Adam, when daily we are confronted, as social beings, by the dolt and the peeve and the minge and the bully, the maniac new Atom? I prefer the attitude of Pepys: "12th, Friday. Up, finding our beds good, but lousy; which made us merry. . . ."

Comic writers can't expect society to be comic just for *them*. "Do you serve women at this bar?" "No," says the barman, "you've got to bring your own." And society to a comic writer is always funny, even, or especially, on its deathbed. People walking into open lift-shafts, being wolfed by lions, missing the swung trapeze, are conventional subjects for a comic draughtsman; and the sight of society falling on its ear, and the prospect of civilisation itself going for a Burton, offer writers possibilities of every kind of laugh. "There is something in the house," said the wife of a comic writer in one of Algernon Blackwood's "John Silence" stories, "that prevents his feeling funny." There's enough, God knows, going on in *our* house to drive Peacock's Prince Seithennyn from drink; but that doesn't prevent a writer from creating a great comic world of his own out of the tragic catastrophe of this. "The best lack all conviction, while the worst are full of passionate intensity," wrote Yeats. But grave, censorious, senatorial, soul-possessing Man, erect on his two spindles, is still a colossal joke. A man in love makes a practical cat laugh. A man in power makes Engels weep—with laughter.

W. W. Jacobs was one of the trimmest, funniest, and most

* These extracts are taken from a broadcast conversation between Thomas and Arthur Calder Marshall.

exact Edwardian writers, whose dialogue is as neat and sly and spare and taut as his mercenary and matrimonial plots. Here, in what I call a *minor* comic world, are the landlubber dreams of sailors on leave, the visions of a pocketful of Bradburys in snug saloons with buxom barmaids. Here are the intricate discomfortures of rival seamen; truculent unpaid rolling-pinned landladies; free fills of baccy; beer on the sly and the nod and the slate. Here all married women are harridans; all widows are plump and comfy and have a little bit put by; all unmarried girls are arch and mysterious; all men without exception are knaves and fools, and very often both, and are solely occupied in strategies concerning money and women and the getting and losing of them.

[*Speaking of Stephen Leacock's works he said:*] I read only his *Sunshine Sketches of a Little Town,* for only in these did Leacock create a *home* for his imagination, a "place" in which *his* people could be born and die, love, fall down, philosophize, have their hair cut, let their hair down, put their feet up.

[*Calder Marshall asked:*] Doesn't P. G. Wodehouse fit your definition of a comic world perfectly?

[*Thomas replied:*] Those chinless, dim, eyeglassed, asinine, bespatted drones were borrowed, lock, stock and title, from memories of the Pink 'Un period and the Smart Set, from the ghostly, hansom past of the moneyed masher and the stage-door johnny. Some people like Jeeves, but include me out: I, for one, do not appreciate gentleman's gentleman's relish.

A truly comic, invented world must live *at the same time* as the world *we* live in.

What does [*present-day comic writing*] amount to? Funny columns in English newspapers, fence-sittings, beachcombings, shymakings; the laboured, witless whimsy and pompous facetiousness of that national institution—or poorhouse of ideas—which the *New Yorker* once called "Paunch." All the best books—or nearly all but the best modern comic books are written by Americans. James Thurber, S. J. Perelman, Frank Sullivan and Robert Benchley, all have written for that brilliant family magazine, but have nothing in common except their superiority to modern English comic journalists.

It is still impossible to compare the shy and baffled, introspective essays, fables, and fabulous reminiscences of Thurber, his cowering terror before the mechanical gadgets, the militant neuroses, the ubiquitous women, the democratic pitfalls and big-business bogies of this modern Americanised Age; it's impossible to compare him, class him, school him, with the glib Groucho zaniness of S. J. Perelman, who writes like a Hollywood advertising copywriter after reading James Joyce, Amanda Ross, Krafft-Ebing, Reverend Spooner, E. E. Cummings and Sam Goldwyn's ace publicity stooge in a state of hypertension in a Turkish bath managed by Man-Mountain Dean. But Thurber, Sullivan, Perelman, Benchley, all excellent comic writers, are all *essayists;* and I am concerned with comic, constructive writers of *stories.* I want, without boisterous backslapping, without the hail-fellow guffaw of the tweedy pipe-sucking tankard-quaffing professional literary comedian, without nudge and titter, without the reedy neigh of the reviewer, I want laughter in books: the sight, and smell, and *sound* of laughter. And almost the only sound I hear from stories now recalls, to me, the sound of the watch in Frances Cornford's poem:

> I thought it said in every tick:
> I am so sick, so sick, so sick;
> O death, come quick, come quick, come quick,
> Come quick, come quick, come quick, come quick.

> (*1948*)

THE ENGLISH FESTIVAL
OF SPOKEN POETRY

There is, in many people, a need to share enthusiasm, which is often expressed in behaviour known, nicely, as "showing off": common to actors, poets, politicians and other trapezists. Many people who read poems like some of them so much that they cannot keep their liking to themselves: they are not content with saying, "Do you know de la Eliot's 'Waste Stranger' or W. H. Houseman's 'A Dog Beneath the Gallows,' isn't it, or aren't they, lovely," but they needs must say, "Listen to this," and reel the lovely stuff off aloud. Sometimes they like the noise their voices make. They find that the words of the poem they reel, familiar and pleasant, acquire a surprising pleasant strangeness when boomed, minced, Keened, crooned, Dyalled or Wolfitted. Known words grow wings; print springs and shoots; the voice discovers the poets' ear; it's found that a poem on a page is only half a poem. And the speakers, realising the inadequacy of their hitherto silent interpretation, sometimes set about learning the business of reading aloud; which is to say, they set about learning the poems which they know by heart, by head and tongue. They put that noise on paper, which is a poem, into their chests and throats, and let it out: they find that good poets are better than they (the readers) thought they were, for crying out loud. And then some of these readers, wanting to show others all that is missed by reading poetry dumb, looked around for an audience.

Families, like countries, take their prophets unkindly, but a verse-speaker in the home is dishonour to be hooted. Show me the family circle that sits in silence while a son or daughter mouths, with gawky zeal, a lyric aloud, and I will recite the whole of *Hudibras* to a weekend convention of moose. These readers cannot rush into the Third Programme at a moment's notice, past the sentinel guard of artists' rifles, disturb the uneven tenor of Tibetan operas and the phalanx of harpsichords. They can found verse-speaking societies in their home places, but who is there to listen except other verse-readers who are only waiting for them to stop? Where can people who like reading poems aloud very much do it? Do it, that is, to a discriminating, enthusiastic, and, on the whole, altruistic audience?

The Oxford Festival of Spoken Poetry was founded twenty years ago, and grew up around the love and care of the late Laurence Binyon. The Festival took place in Oxford until the outbreak of the last never-to-be-repeated war. Now it is conducted in London, but its committee and their supporters hope soon to be able to return to Oxford. The Festival of Spoken Poetry is run by poets. Nearly all the judges are poets; poets—men who work hard at another job in order to be able to work hard at the job they really like when they're not working. The judges of the Festival: cool (specially now), impersonal, knowledgeable, mature, lofty uncompromising not-to-be-bribed-or-trifled-with ascetic remote creatures who (if only the competitors could know—and I speak for the masculine judges alone) sit there in their perspiring glory, thinking of cricket and ice and legs, their little hearts thumping among so many summery flowered dresses, bright smiles, untrammelled youth, high heels, endeavour, scent and zeal.

It may perhaps be thought that I am frivolling about what is, really, a most sincere, conscientious and extremely able Festival. But it *is* a Festival. It is not a cold competition. It runs for four days every year, and it is to be enjoyed. We all enjoy it, competitors, judges, carpers, audience and all. There were over 300 people this year, from all over the country, who stood up and read Marlowe, Tennyson, Sidney Keyes, Pope, mostly because they love reading poetry aloud and here was the place and the time to read it with no strings or nonsense. This is no Phil the High-Falutin's Ball, but a Festival of and for unfrumpish, unfreakish, sane people with voices. When a competitor is not reading, he or she is listening to the others read: and listenng with a knowledgeable liking.

I'm not going to say that all the readers are first class. This is a Festival and an amateur competition, not a professional day-out for successful exhibitionists. Many of the competitors would wish to become full-time actors, readers, broadcasters; a few may be. Like everything that is any good, this Festival is full of faults.

I think that the readers should be allowed, if they want to, to have, in front of them, the text of the poems they are reading. I thought that when a *long* poem came up to be read, some of the competitors very dully overslowed their reading because they had too much to remember and were, all too obviously, feeling for the next verse. I thought that some of the "judgments" had to be made too hastily, so that a tepid, but finished, reading was likely to be valued higher than a true, warm but hesitant, occasionally blundering, one.

Many readings were plagued with the more obvious sicknesses of reading-aloud: insistent sibilance, the, for want of a better phrase, "Old Vic" voice: an affected inflecting that strangles rhythm and truncheons meaning. There was the "dead voice": a way of speaking that pretends to emphasise the importance of flat understatement only because the abilty to *give* isn't there. The smile, not the voice, beautiful: the suppositon of an arch, nudging connivance between speaker and listener; the attitude of "*We* know, though the others don't." There was, though rarely, the *acting* of the spoken, the taught, but never taut, gesture to illustrate an unillustratable, except by inflection, point or temper of a line, the starry-eyed horizon-searching, the mechanical hand-work of simulated passion, like a soprano milking a goat.

But oh so rare. Nearly everyone, nearly *everyone,* enjoyed this Festival as it has been enjoyed for twenty years. No humbug. No Slade-fringed or tennis-party voice, no hairy crank with a jaeger lilt or a maypole accent, no henna'd and bangled New-Lifing. And the standard of the reading was extremely high. Poems are written in lines, and if you shut your eyes, which was some-times difficult to do, you could hear, with no jarring of brakes, where the lines stopped. You could *hear.*

(1948)

ON READING ONE'S OWN POEMS

To choose what I should read tonight, I looked through seventy odd poems of mine, and found that many *are* odd indeed and that some may be poems. And I decided not to choose those that strike me, still, as pretty peculiar, but to stick to a few of the ones that do move a little way towards the state and destination I imagine I intended to be theirs when, in small rooms in Wales, arrogantly and devotedly I began them.

For I like to think that the poems most narrowly odd are among those I wrote earliest, and that the later poems are wider and deeper—though Time, if interested, may well prove me wrong, and find that the reverse is true, or that each statement is false.

I do not remember—that is the point—the first impulse that pumped and shoved most of the earlier poems along, and they are still too near to me, with their vehement beat-pounding black and green rhythms like those of a very young policeman exploding, for me to see the written evidence of it. My interpretation of them —if that is not too weighty a word just for reading them aloud and trying to give some idea of their sound and shape—could only be a parroting of the say that I once had.

"And all that a reader-aloud of his own poems can hope to do is to try to put across his own memory of the original impulses behind his poems, deepening, maybe, and if only for a moment, the inner meaning of the words on the printed pages."

How I wish I could agree wholeheartedly with that, let alone hope to achieve it! But, oh, the danger! For what a reader-aloud of his own poems so often does, is to mawken or melo-dramatise them, making a single simple phrase break with the fears or throb with the terrors from which he deludes himself the phrase has been born.

There is the other reader, of course, who manages, by studious flatness, semidetachment, and an almost condescending undersaying of his poems, to give the impression that what he really means is: Great things, but my own.

That I belong to the very *dangerous* first group of readers will be only to clear.

The first poem is titled by its first line:

THERE WAS A SAVIOUR

There was a saviour
Rarer than radium,
Commoner than water, crueller than truth
Children kept from the sun
Assembled at his tongue
To hear the golden note turn in a groove,
Prisoners of wishes locked their eyes
In the jails and studies of his keyless smiles.

The voice of children says
From a lost wilderness
There was calm to be done in his safe unrest,
When hindering man hurt
Man, animal, or bird
We hid our fears in that murdering breath,
Silence, silence to do, when earth grew loud,
In lairs and asylums of the tremendous shout.

There was glory to hear
In the churches of his tears,
Under his downy arm you sighed as he struck,
O you who could not cry
On to the ground when a man died
Put a tear for joy in the unearthly flood
And laid your cheek against a cloud-formed shell:
Now in the dark there is only yourself and myself.

Two proud, blacked brothers cry,
Winter-locked side by side,
To this inhospitable hollow year,
O we who could not stir
One lean sigh when we heard
Greed on man beating near and fire neighbour
But wailed and nested in the sky-blue wall
Now break a giant tear for the little known fall,

For the drooping of homes
That did not nurse our bones,
Brave deaths of only ones but never found,
Now see, alone in us,
Our own true strangers' dust
Ride through the doors of our unentered house.
Exiled in us we arouse the soft,
Unclenched, armless, silk and rough love that breaks all rocks.

The next poem tells of a mother and her child who is about to be born. It is not a narrative, nor an argument, but a series of conflicting images which move through pity and violence to an unreconciled acceptance of suffering: the mother's *and* the child's. This poem has been called obscure. I refuse to believe that it is obscurer than pity, violence, or suffering. But being a poem, not a lifetime, it is more compressed:

'IF MY HEAD HURT A HAIR'S FOOT'

'If my head hurt a hair's foot
Pack back the downed bone. If the unpricked ball of my breath
Bump on a spout let the bubbles jump out.
Sooner drop with the worm of the ropes round my throat
Than bully ill love in the clouted scene.

'All game phrases fit your ring of a cockfight:
I'll comb the snared woods with a glove on a lamp,
Peck, sprint, dance on fountains and duck time
Before I rush in a crouch the ghost with a hammer, air,
Strike light, and bloody a loud room.

'If my bunched, monkey coming is cruel
Rage me back to the making house. My hand unravel
When you sew the deep door. The bed is a cross place.
Bend, if my journey ache, direction like an arc or make
A limp and riderless shape to leap nine thinning months.'

'No. Not for Christ's dazzling bed
Or a nacreous sleep among soft particles and charms
My dear would I change my tears or your iron head.

Thrust, my daughter or son, to escape, there is none, none, none,
Nor when all ponderous heaven's host of waters breaks.

'Now to awake husked of gestures and my joy like a cave
To the anguish and carrion, to the infant forever unfree,
O my lost love bounced from a good home;
The grain that hurries this way from the rim of the grave
Has a voice and a house, and there and here you must couch and
   cry.

'Rest beyond choice in the dust-appointed grain,
At the breast stored with seas. No return
Through the waves of the fat streets nor the skeleton's thin ways.
The grave and my calm body are shut to your coming as stone,
And the endless beginning of prodigies suffers open.'

Reading one's own poems aloud is letting the cat out of the
bag. You may have always suspected bits of a poem to be over-
weighted, overviolent, or daft, and then, suddenly, with the poet's
tongue around them, your suspicion is made certain. How he
slows up a line to savour it, remembering what trouble it took,
once upon a time, to make it just so, at the very moment, you may
think, when the poem needs crispness and speed. Does the cat
snarl or mew the better when its original owner—or father, even,
the tom poet—lets it out of the bag, than when another does, who
never put it in?

POEM IN OCTOBER

It was my thirtieth year to heaven
Woke to my hearing from harbour and neighbour wood
     And the mussel pooled and the heron
          Priested shore
     The morning beckon
With water praying and call of seagull and rook
And the knock of sailing boats on the net webbed wall
          Myself to set foot
          That second
     In the still sleeping town and set forth.

My birthday began with the water-
Birds and the birds of the winged trees flying my name
    Above the farms and the white horses
        And I rose
        In rainy autumn
And walked abroad in a shower of all my days.
High tide and the heron dived when I took the road
        Over the border
        And the gates
    Of the town closed as the town awoke.

    A springful of larks in a rolling
Cloud and the roadside bushes brimming with whistling
    Blackbirds and the sun of October
        Summery
        On the hill's shoulder,
Here were fond climates and sweet singers suddenly
Come in the morning where I wandered and listened
        To the rain wringing
        Wind blow cold
    In the wood faraway under me.

    Pale rain over the dwindling harbour
And over the sea wet church the size of a snail
    With its horns through mist and the castle
        Brown as owls
        But all the gardens
Of spring and summer were blooming in the tall tales
Beyond the border and under the lark full cloud.
        There could I marvel
        My birthday
    Away but the weather turned around.

    It turned away from the blithe country
And down the other air and the blue altered sky
    Streamed again a wonder of summer
        With apples
        Pears and red currants
And I saw in the turning so clearly a child's
Forgotten mornings when he walked with his mother

Through the parables
    Of sun light
And the legends of the green chapels

And the twice told fields of infancy
That his tears burned my cheeks and his heart moved in mine.
    These were the woods the river and sea
        Where a boy
        In the listening
Summertime of the dead whispered the truth of his joy
To the trees and the stones and the fish in the tide.
    And the mystery
        Sang alive
Still in the water and singingbirds.

And there could I marvel my birthday
Away but the weather turned around. And the true
    Joy of the long dead child sang burning
        In the sun.
    It was my thirtieth
Year to heaven stood there then in the summer noon
Though the town below lay leaved with October blood.
    O may my heart's truth
        Still be sung
On this high hill in a year's turning.

The next poem I'll read is the only one I have written that
is, directly, about the life and death of one particular human
being I knew—and not about the very many lives and deaths
whether seen, as in my first poems, in the tumultuous world of
my own being or, as in the later poems, in war, grief, and the
great holes and corners of universal love.

AFTER THE FUNERAL

(In memory of Ann Jones)

After the funeral, mule praises, brays,
Windshake of sailshaped ears, muffle-toed tap
Tap happily of one peg in the thick
Grave's foot, blinds down the lids, the teeth in black,

The spittled eyes, the salt ponds in the sleeves,
Morning smack of the spade that wakes up sleep,
Shakes a desolate boy who slits his throat
In the dark of the coffin and sheds dry leaves,
That breaks one bone to light with a judgment clout,
After the feast of tear-stuffed time and thistles
In a room with a stuffed fox and a stale fern,
I stand, for this memorial's sake, alone
In the snivelling hours with dead, humped Ann
Whose hooded, fountain heart once fell in puddles
Round the parched worlds of Wales and drowned each sun
(Though this for her is a monstrous image blindly
Magnified out of praise; her death was a still drop;
She would not have me sinking in the holy
Flood of her heart's fame; she would lie dumb and deep
And need no druid of her broken body).
But I, Ann's bard on a raised hearth, call all
The seas to service that her wood-tongued virtue
Babble like a bellbuoy over the hymning heads,
Bow down the walls of the ferned and foxy woods
That her love sing and swing through a brown chapel,
Bless her bent spirit with four, crossing birds.
Her flesh was meek as milk, but this skyward statue
With the wild breast and blessed and giant skull
Is carved from her in a room with a wet window
In a fiercely mourning house in a crooked year.
I know her scrubbed and sour humble hands
Lie with religion in their cramp, her threadbare
Whisper in a damp word, her wits drilled hollow,
Her fist of a face died clenched on a round pain;
And sculptured Ann is seventy years of stone.
These cloud-sopped, marble hands, this monumental
Argument of the hewn voice, gesture and psalm,
Storm me forever over her grave until
The stuffed lung of the fox twitch and cry Love
And the strutting fern lay seeds on the black sill.

(1949)

THREE POEMS

"In Country Sleep" appeared first in a magazine which raised its hands in despair of philistine apathy so beseechingly high and so often it has since lain down from fatigue, and in a limited edition, ten copies of which are on vellum, available only to the rich who should be spending what is left of their time slimming for the eye of the needle.

"Over Sir John's Hill" has been printed in a handsome and richly appointed palace of a quarterly erected in Rome. "In the White Giant's Thigh" is in manuscript, waiting for someone who prints strikingly few copies, at impossible prices, on fine soft Cashmere goat's hair.

These three poems will, one day, form separate parts of a long poem which is in preparation: that is to say, some of the long poem is written down on paper, some of it is in a rough draft in the head, and the rest of it radiantly unworded in ambitious conjecture.

A miscellaneous writer, such as myself, who is prepared to sit in front of this cold utensil and talk, in public confidence, about his new long unwritten poem, deserves to be a successful man of letters. I used to think that once a writer became a man of letters, if only for half an hour, he was done for. And here am I now, at the very *moment* of such an odious, though respectable, danger.

Perhaps, after this, I shall become transformed into establishment; all my old doubts and worries will be over; I need bother my head about nothing except birth, death, sex, money, politics and religion, and, jowled and wigged, aloof as a bloodhound, I may summon my former literary delinquence before me and give it a long, periodic sentence.

What can I say about the plan of a long "poem in preparation"—I hope the quotation marks come stinging across this, to me, unbelievable lack of wires, like peeved bees—that can interest anyone save, vaguely, myself and of course my guardian angel, a failed psychoanalyst in this life who is even now prodnosing in the air above me, casebook in claw, a little seedy and down-at-winged-heel, in the guttural consulting-rooms of space? What can I say about this long poem-to-be except that the plan of it is grand and simple and that the grandeur will seem, to many, to be purple and grandiose and the simplicity crude and sentimental? The poem is to be called "In Country Heaven." The godhead, the author, the milky-way farmer, the first cause, architect, lamp-lighter, quintessence, the beginning Word, the anthropomorphic bowler-out and blackballer, the stuff of all men, scapegoat, martyr, maker, woe-bearer—He, on top of a hill in Heaven, weeps whenever, outside that state of being called his country, one of his worlds drops dead, vanishes screaming, shrivels, explodes, murders itself. And, when he weeps, Light and His tears glide down together, hand in hand. So, at the beginning of the projected poem, he weeps, and Country Heaven is suddenly dark. Bushes and owls blow out like candles. And the countrymen of heaven crouch all together under the hedges and, among themselves in the tear-salt darkness, surmise which world, which star, which of their late, turning homes, in the skies has gone for ever. And this time, spreads the heavenly hedgerow rumour, it is the Earth. The Earth has killed itself. It is black, petrified, wizened, poisoned, burst; insanity has blown it rotten; and on creatures at all, joyful, despairing, cruel, kind, dumb, afire, loving, dull, shortly and brutishly hunt their days down like enemies on that corrupted face. And, one by one, these heavenly hedgerow-men, who once were of the Earth, call one another, through the long night, Light and His tears falling, what they remember, what they sense in the submerged wilderness and on the exposed hairsbreadth of the mind, what they feel trembling on the nerves of a nerve, what they know in their Edenie hearts, of that self-called place. They remember places, fears, loves, exultation, misery, animal joy, ignorance and mysteries, all *we* know and do not know.

The poem is made of these tellings. And the poem becomes, at last, an affirmation of the beautiful and terrible worth of the Earth. It grows into a praise of what is and what could be on this lump in the skies. It is a poem about happiness.

I do not expect that a first hearing of the three separate poems I am going to read can give any idea of how and where they will, eventually, take their places, in that lofty, pretentious, down-to-earth-and-into-the-secrets, optimistic, ludicrous, knock-me-down moony scheme. I do not yet know myself their relevance to the whole, hypothetical structure. But I do know they belong to it.

The remembered tellings, which are the components of the poem, are not all told as though they are remembered; the poem will not be a series of poems in the past tense. The memory, in all tenses, can look towards the future, can caution and admonish. The rememberer may live himself back into active participation in the remembered scene, adventure, or spiritual condition.

"Over Sir John's Hill." Sir John's Hill is a real hill overlooking an estuary in West Wales.

Over Sir John's hill,
The hawk on fire hangs still;
In a hoisted cloud, at drop of dusk, he pulls to his claws
And gallows, up the rays of his eyes the small birds of the bay
And the shrill child's play
Wars
Of the sparrows and such who swansing, dusk, in wrangling
      hedges.
And blithely they squawk
To fiery tyburn over the wrestle of elms until
The flash the noosed hawk
Crashes, and slowly the fishing holy stalking heron
In the river Towy below bows his tilted headstone.

Flash, and the plumes crack,
And a black cap of jack-
Daws Sir John's just hill dons, and again the gulled birds hare
To the hawk on fire, the halter height, over Towy's fins,
In a whack of wind.
There
Where the elegiac fisherbird stabs and paddles
In the pebbly dab-filled
Shallow and sedge, and 'dilly dilly,' calls the loft hawk,
'Come and be killed,'
I open the leaves of the water at a passage
Of psalms and shadows among the pincered sandcrabs prancing

And read, in a shell,
Death clear as a buoy's bell:
All praise of the hawk on fire in hawk-eyed dusk be sung,
When his viperish fuse hangs looped with flames under the brand
Wing, and blest shall
Young
Green chickens of the bay and bushes cluck, 'dilly dilly,
Come let us die.'
We grieve as the blithe birds, never again, leave shingle and elm,
The heron and I,
I young Aesop fabling to the near night by the dingle
Of eels, saint heron hymning in the shell-hung distant

Crystal harbour vale
Where the sea cobbles sail,
And wharves of water where the walls dance and the white cranes
    stilt.
It is the heron and I, under judging Sir John's elmed
Hill, tell-tale the knelled
Guilt
Of the led-astray birds whom God, for their breast of whistles,
Have mercy on,
God in his whirlwind silence save, who marks the sparrows hail
For their souls' song.
Now the heron grieves in the weeded verge. Through windows
Of dusk and water I see the tilting whispering

Heron, mirrored, go,
As the snapt feathers snow,
Fishing in the tear of the Towy. Only a hoot owl
Hollows, a grassblade blown in cupped hands, in the looted elms
And no green cocks or hens
Shout
Now on Sir John's hill. The heron, ankling the scaly
Lowlands of the waves,
Makes all the music; and I who hear the tune of the slow,
Wear-willow river, grave,
Before the lunge of the night, the notes on this time-shaken
Stone for the sake of the souls of the slain birds sailing.

"In the White Giant's Thigh," just written, will no doubt, have many small details altered before it is printed, but the general feel and sound of it will remain the same even when I have cleared up some of its more obviously overlush, arch and exuberant, mauve gauche moments.

IN THE WHITE GIANT'S THIGH

Through throats where many rivers meet, the curlews cry,
Under the conceiving moon, on the high chalk hill,
And there this night I walk in the white giant's thigh
Where barren as boulders women lie longing still

To labour and love though they lay down long ago.

Through throats where many rivers meet, the women pray,
Pleading in the waded bay for the seed to flow
Though the names on their weed grown stones are rained away,

And alone in the night's eternal, curving act
They yearn with tongues of curlews for the unconceived
And immemorial sons of the cudgelling, hacked

Hill. Who once in gooseskin winter loved all ice leaved
In the courters' lanes, or twined in the ox roasting sun
In the wains tonned so high that the wisps of the hay
Clung to the pitching clouds, or gay with any one
Young as they in the after milking moonlight lay
Under the lighted shapes of faith and their moonshade
Petticoats galed high, or shy with the rough riding boys,
Now clasp me to their grains in the gigantic glade,

Who once, green countries since, were a hedgerow of joys.
Time by, their dust was flesh the swineherd rooted sly,
Flared in the reek of the wiving sty with the rush
Light of his thighs, spreadeagle to the dunghill sky,
Or with their orchard man in the core of the sun's bush
Rough as cows' tongues and thrashed with brambles their buttermilk
Manes, under his quenchless summer barbed gold to the bone,

Or rippling soft in the spinney moon as the silk
And ducked and draked white lake that harps to a hail stone.

Who once were a bloom of wayside brides in the hawed house
And heard the lewd, wooed field flow to the coming frost,
The scurrying, furred small friars squeal, in the dowse
Of day, in the thistle aisles, till the white owl crossed
Their breast, the vaulting does roister, the horned bucks climb
Quick in the wood at love, where a torch of foxes foams,
All birds and beasts of the linked night uproar and chime

And the mole snout blunt under his pilgrimage of domes,
Or, butter fat goosegirls, bounced in a gambo bed,
Their breasts full of honey, under their gander king
Trounced by his wings in the hissing shippen, long dead
And gone that barley dark where their clogs danced in the spring,
And their firefly hairpins flew, and the ricks ran round—

(But nothing bore, no mouthing babe to the veined hives
Hugged, and barren and bare on Mother Goose's ground
They with the simple Jacks were a boulder of wives)—

Now curlew cry me down to kiss the mouths of their dust.
The dust of their kettles and clocks swings to and fro
Where the hay rides now or the bracken kitchens rust
As the arc of the billhooks that flashed the hedges low
And cut the birds' boughs that the minstrel sap ran red.
They from houses where the harvest kneels, hold me hard,
Who heard the tall bell sail down the Sundays of the dead
And the rain wring out its tongues on the faded yard,
Teach me the love that is evergreen after the fall leaved
Grave, after Belovéd on the grass gulfed cross is scrubbed
Off by the sun and Daughters no longer grieved
Save by their long desirers in the fox cubbed
Streets or hungering in the crumbled wood: to these
Hale dead and deathless do the women of the hill
Love for ever meridian through the courters' trees

And the daughters of darkness flame like Fawkes fires still.

(*1950*)

REPLIES TO AN ENQUIRY*

1. Do you intend your poetry to be useful to yourself or others?

   To both. Poetry is the rhythmic, inevitably narrative, movement from an overclothed blindness to a naked vision that
   depends in its intensity on the strength of the labour put into
   the creation of the poetry. My poetry is, or should be, useful
   to me for one reason: it is the record of my individual struggle
   from darkness towards some measure of light, and what of the
   individual struggle is still to come benefits by the sight and
   knowledge of the faults and fewer merits in that concrete
   record. My poetry is, or should be, useful to others for its
   individual recording of that same struggle with which they
   are necessarily acquainted.

2. Do you think there can now be a use for narrative poetry?

   Yes. Narrative is essential. Much of the flat, abstract poetry
   of the present has no narrative movement, no movement at all,
   and is consequently dead. There must be a progressive line,
   or theme, of movement in every poem. The more subjective
   a poem, the clearer the narrative line. Narrative, in its widest
   sense, satisfies what Eliot, talking of "meaning," calls "one
   habit of the reader." Let the narrative take that one logical
   habit of the reader along with its movement, and the essence
   of the poem will do its work on him.

3. Do you wait for a spontaneous impulse before writing a poem;
   if so, is this impulse verbal or visual?

   No. The writing of a poem is, to me, the physical and mental
   task of constructing a formally watertight compartment of
   words, preferably with a main moving column (*i.e.*, narrative)

* These replies to questions submitted by the editor were published in
New Verse, October, 1934.

to hold a little of the real causes and forces of the creative brain and body. The causes and forces are always there, and always need a concrete expression. To me, the poetical "impulse" or "inspiration" is only the sudden, and generally physical, coming of energy to the constructional, craftsman ability. The laziest workman receives the fewest impulses. And vice versa.

4. Have you been influenced by Freud and how do you regard him?

Yes. Whatever is hidden should be made naked. To be stripped of darkness is to be clean, to strip of darkness is to make clean. Poetry, recording the stripping of the individual darkness, must, inevitably, cast light upon what has been hidden for too long, and, by so doing, make clean the naked exposure. Freud cast light on a little of the darkness he had exposed. Benefiting by the sight of the light and the knowledge of the hidden nakedness, poetry must drag further into the clean nakedness of light more even of the hidden causes than Freud could realise.

5. Do you take your stand with any political or politico-economic party or creed?

I take my stand with any revolutionary body that asserts it to be the right of all men to share, equally and impartially, every production of man from man and from the source of production at man's disposal, for only through such an essentially revolutionary body can there be the possibility of a communal art.

6. As a poet what distinguishes you, do you think, from an ordinary man?

Only the use of the medium of poetry to express the causes and forces which are the same in all men.

ON POETRY

I agree that music-hall songs can be good poetry—so can limericks, drawing- or a taproom—but I don't think cracker-mottoes, etc., ever have been. I think, Stephens,* you must be pulling my (comparatively) young leg. The younger generation used to be called, by their elders, flippant. Not any longer. It's we, now, who deprecate their flippancy. I feel rather like the little pedantically reproving girl addressing Matthew Arnold in Max Beerbohm's picture: "Why, Uncle Matthew, oh why, will not you be always wholly serious?" I'm all for taking the *serious* nonsense out of one's appreciation of poetry; I hate, as much as you do, the hushed voice and hats-off attitude, but I don't like the double-bluffing approach that pretends to think that "I'm one of the ruins that Cromwell knocked about a bit" is better poetry than, say, the serious, unfashionable work of Cowper or Francis Thompson. It's just very different poetry. . . .

Almost anything one says about poetry is as true and important as *anything* else that *anyone* else has said. Some people react *physically* to the magic of poetry, to the moments, that is, of authentic revelation, of the communication, the *sharing*, at its highest level, of personal experience; they say they feel a twanging at their tear ducts, or a prickling of the scalp, or a tickling of the spine, or tremors in what they hope is their heart. Others say that they have a kind of a sort of a vague feeling somewhere that "this is the real stuff." Others claim that their "purely aesthetic emotion" was induced by certain assonances and alliterations. And some are content merely to say, as they said of the first cinematographic picture, "By God, it moves." And so, of course, by God, it does, for that is another name for the magic beyond definition. . . .

The magic in a poem is always accidental. No poet would

* James Stephens. These excerpts are taken from a discussion with Stephens on poetry, which was broadcast by the B.B.C.

labour intensively upon the intricate craft of poetry unless he hoped that, suddenly, the accident of magic would occur. He *has* to agree with Chesterton that the miraculous thing about miracles is that they *do* sometimes happen. And the best poem is that whose worked-upon unmagical passages come closest, in texture and intensity, to those moments of magical accident. . . .

And there's this to be said, too. Poetry, to a poet, is the most rewarding work in the world. A good poem is a contribution to reality. The world is never the same once a good poem has been added to it. A good poem helps to change the shape and significance of the universe, helps to extend everyone's knowledge of himself and the world around him. . . .

I think there's an inverted snobbery—and a suggestion of bad logic—in being proud of the fact that one's poems sell very badly. *Of course,* nearly *every* poet wants his poems to be read by as many people as possible. Craftsmen don't put their products in the attic. And contempt for the public, which is composed of potential readers, is contempt for the profound usefulness of your own craft. Go on thinking that you don't *need* to be read, and you'll find that it may become quite true: no one *will* feel the need to read it, because it is written for yourself alone; and the public won't feel any impulse to gate-crash such a private party. Moreover, to take no notice of the work of your contemporaries is to disregard a whole *vital* part of the world you live in, and necessarily to devitalise your own work: to narrow its scope and possibilities: to be half dead as you write. . . .

What's more, a poet is a poet for such a very tiny bit of his life; for the rest, he is a human being, one of whose responsibilities is to know and feel, as much as he can, all that is moving around and within him, so that his poetry, when he comes to write it, can be his attempt at an expression of the summit of man's experience on this very peculiar and, in 1946, this apparently hell-bent earth.

(*1946*)

HOW TO BE A POET

OR

THE ASCENT OF PARNASSUS MADE EASY

Let me, at once, make it clear that I am not considering, in these supposedly informative jottings, Poetry as an Art or a Craft, as the rhythmic verbal expression of a spiritual necessity or urge, but solely as the means to a social end; that end being the achievement of a status in society solid enough to warrant the poet discarding and expunging those affectations, so essential in the early stages, of speech, dress, and behaviour; an income large enough to satisfy his physical demands, unless he has already fallen victim to the Poet's Evil, or Great Wen; and a permanent security from the fear of having to write any more. I do not intend to ask, let alone to answer, the question, "Is Poetry a Good Thing?" but only, "Can Poetry Be Made Good Business?"

I shall, to begin with, introduce to you a few of the main types of poets who have made the social and financial grade.

First, though not in order of importance, is the poet who has emerged docketed "lyrical," from the Civil Service. He can be divided, so far as his physical appearance goes, into two types. He is either thin, not to say of a shagged-out appearance, with lips as fulsome, sensual, and inviting as a hen's ovipositor, bald from all too maculate birth, his eyes made small and reddened by reading books in French, a language he cannot understand, in an attic in the provinces while young and repellent, his voice like the noise of a mouse's nail on tinfoil, his nostrils transparent, his breath grey; or else he is jowled and bushy, with curved pipe and his nose full of dottle, the look of all Sussex in his stingo'd eyes, his burry tweeds smelling of the dogs he loathes, with a voice like a literate airedale's that has learned its vowels by correspondence course, and an intimate friend of Chesterton's, whom he never met.

Let us see in what manner our man has arrived at his present and enviable position as the Poet who has made Poetry Pay.

Dropped into the Civil Service at an age when many of our young poets now are running away to Broadcasting House, today's equivalent of the Sea, he is at first lost to sight in the mountains of red tape which, in future years, he is so mordantly, though with a wry and puckered smile, to dismiss in a paragraph in his "Around and About My Shelves." After a few years, he begins to peer out from the forms and files in which he leads his ordered, nibbling life, and picks up a cheese crumb here, a dropping there, in his ink-stained thumbs. His ears are uncannily sensitive: he can hear an opening being opened a block of offices away.

And soon he learns that a poem in a Civil Service magazine is, if not a step up the ladder, at least a lick in the right direction. And he writes a poem. It is, of course, about Nature; it confesses a wish to escape from humdrum routine and embrace the unsophisticated life of the farm laborer; he desires, though without scandal, to wake up with the birds; he expresses the opinion that a plowshare, not a pen, best fits his little strength; a decorous pantheist, he is one with the rill, the rhyming mill, the rosy-bottomed milkmaid, the russet-cheeked rat-catcher, swains, swine, pipits, pippins. You can smell the country in his poems, the fields, the flowers, the armpits of Triptolemus, the barns, the byres, the hay, and, most of all, the corn. The poem is published. A single lyrical extract from the beginning must suffice:—

> The roaring street is hushed!
> Hushed, do I say?
> The wing of a bird has brushed
> Time's cobwebs away.
> Still, still as death, the air
> Over the grey stones!
> And over the grey thoroughfare
> I hear—sweet tones!—
> A blackbird open its bill,
> —A blackbird, aye!—
> And sing its liquid fill
> From the London sky.

A little time after the publication of the poem, he is nodded to in the corridor by Hotchkiss of Inland Revenue, himself a weekending poet with two slim volumes to his credit, half an inch in the Poets' Who's Who or the Newbolt Calendar, an ambitious wife with a vee-neck and a fringe who lost the battle of the Slade, a small car that always drives, as though by itself, to Sussex—as a parson's horse would once unthinkingly trot to the public house—and an unfinished monograph on the influence of Blunden on the hedgerow.

Hotchkiss, lunching with Sowerby of Customs, himself a literary figure of importance with a weekly column in Will o' Lincoln's Weekly and his name on the editorial list of the Masterpiece of the Fortnight Club (volumes at reduced rates to all writers, and a complete set of the works of Mary Webb quarter-price at Christmas), says casually, "You've rather a promising fellow in your department, Sowerby. Young Cribbe. I've been reading a little thing of his, 'I Desire the Curlew.'" And Cribbe's name goes the small, foetid rounds.

He is next asked to contribute a *group* of poems to Hotch-kiss's anthology, "New Pipes," which Sowerby praises—"a rare gift for the haunting phrase"—in Will o' Lincoln's. Cribbe sends copies of the anthology, each laboriously signed, "To the greatest living English poet, in homage," to twenty of the dullest poets still on their hind legs. Some of his inscribed gifts are acknowledged. Sir Tom Knight spares a few generous, though bemused, moments to scribble a message on a sheet of crested writing paper removed, during a never-to-be-repeated weekend visit, from a shortsighted but not all that shortsighted peer. "Dear Mr. Crabbe," Sir Tom writes, "I appreciate your little tribute. Your poem, 'Nocturne with Lilies,' is worthy of Shanks. Go on. Go on. There is room on the mount." The fact that Cribbe's poem is not "Nocturne with Lilies" at all, but "On Hearing Delius by a Lych-Gate," does not perturb Cribbe, who carefully files the letter, after blowing away the dandruff, and soon is in the throes of collecting his poems together to make, *misericordia,* a book, "Linnet and Spindle," dedicated "To Clem Sowerby, that green-fingered gardener in the Gardens of the Hesperides."

The book appears. Some favourable notice is taken, particularly in Middlesex. And Sowerby, too modest to review it himself after such a gratifying dedication, reviews it under a different name. "This young poet," he writes, "is not, thanks be it, too 'modernistic' to pay reverence to the shining source of his inspiration. Cribbe will go far."

And Cribbe goes to his publishers. A contract is drawn up, Messrs. Stitch and Time undertaking to publish his next book of verse on condition that they have the first option on his next nine novels. He contrives also to be engaged as a casual reader of manuscripts to Messrs. Stitch and Time, and returns home clutching a parcel which contains a book on the Development of the Oxford Movement in Finland by a Cotswold Major, three blank-verse tragedies about Mary Queen of Scots, and a novel entitled "Tomorrow, Jennifer."

Now Cribbe, until his contract, has never thought of writing a novel. But, undaunted by the fact that he cannot tell one person from another—people, to him, are all one dull, grey mass, except celebrities and departmental superiors—that he has no interest whatsoever in anything they do or say, except in so far as it concerns his career, and that his inventive resources are as limited as those of a chipmunk on a treadmill, he sits down in his shirt-sleeves, loosens his collar, thumbs in the shag, and begins to study in earnest how best, with no qualifications, to make a success of commercial fiction. He soon comes to the conclusion that only quick sales and ephemeral reputations are made by tough novels with such titles as "I've Got It Coming" or "Ten Cents a Dice," by proletarian novels about the conversion to dialectical materialism of Palais-de wide boys, entitled, maybe, "Red Rain on You, Alf," by novels, called, maybe, "Melody in Clover," about dark men with slight limps, called Dirk Conway and their love for two women, lascivious Ursula Mountclare and little, shy Fay Waters. And he soon sees that only the smallest sales, and notices only in the loftiest monthlies of the most limited circulation, will ever result from his writing such a novel as "The Inner Zodiac," by G. H. Q. Bidet, a ruthless analysis of the ideological conflicts arising from the relationship between Philip Armour, an international impotent physicist, Tristram Wolf, a bisexual sculptor in teak, and Philip's virginal but dynamic Creole wife, Titania, a lecturer in Balkan Economics, and how these highly sensitised characters—so redolent, as they are, of the post-Sartre Age—react a profound synthesis while working together, for the sake of Oneness, in a Unesco Clinic.

No fool, Cribbe realises, even in the early stages of his exploration, with theodolite and respirator through darkest Foyle, that the novel to write is that which commands a steady, unsensational, provincial and suburban sale and concerns, for choice, the birth, education, financal ups-and-downs, marriages, separations, and deaths of five generations of a family of Lancashire cotton-brokers. This novel, he grasps at once, should be in the form of a trilogy, and each volume should bear some such solid, uneventful title as "The Warp," "The Woof," and "The Way." And he sets to work.

From the reviews of Cribbe's first novel, one may select: "Here is sound craftsmanship allied to sterling characterisation." "Incidents a-plenty." "You become as familiar with George Steadiman, his wife Muriel, old Tobias Matlock (a delightful vignette) and all the inhabitants of Loom House, as you do with your own family." "These dour Northcotes grow on you." "English as Manchester rain." "Mr. Cribbe is a bull-terrier." "A story in the Phyllis Bottome class."

On the success of the novel, Cribbe joins the N.I.B. Club, delivers a paper on the Early Brett Young Country, and becomes a regular reviewer, praising every other novel he receives—("The prose shimmers")—and inviting every third novelist to dine at the Servile Club, to which he has recently been elected.

When the whole of the trilogy has appeared, Cribbe rises, like scum, to the N.I.B. committee, attends all the memorial services for men of letters who are really dead for the first time in fifty years, tears up his old contract and signs another, brings out a new novel, which becomes a Book Society choice, is offered, by Messrs. Stitch and Time, a position in an "advisory capacity," which he accepts, leaves the Civil Service, buys a cottage in Bucks ("You wouldn't think it was only thirty miles from London, would you. Look, old man, see that crested grebe." A starling flies by), a new desk and a secretary whom he later marries for her touch-typing. Poetry? Perhaps a sonnet in the *Sunday Times* every now and then; a little collection of verse once in a while ("My first love, you know"). But it doesn't really bother him any more, though it got him where he is. *He has made the grade!*

2

And now we must move to see, for a moment, a very different kind of poet, whom we shall call Cedric. To follow in Cedric's footsteps—(he'd love you to, and would never call a policeman unless it was that frightfully sinister sergeant you see sometimes in Mecklenburgh Square, just like an El Greco)—you must be born twilightly into the middle classes, go to one of the correct schools—(which, of course, you must loathe, for it is essential, from the first, to be misunderstood)—and arrive at the University with your reputation already established as a coming poet and looking, if possible, something between a Guards Officer and a fashionable photographer's doxy.

You may say, But how is one to arrive with one's reputation already established as "a poet to watch"? (Poet-watching may in the future become as popular as bird-watching. And it is quite reasonable to imagine the editorial offices of "The Poetaster" being bought up by the nation as a sanctuary.) But that is a question outside the scope of these all-too-rough notes, as it must be assumed that anyone wishing to take up Poetry as a career has always known how to turn the stuff out when required. And also Cedric's college tutor was his housemaster's best friend. So here is Cedric, known already to the discerning few for his sensitive poems about golden limbs, sun-jeweled fronds, the ambrosia of the first shy kiss in the delicate-traceried caverns of the moon (really the school boot-cupboard), at the threshold of fame and the world laid out before him like a row of balletomanes.

If this were the twenties, Cedric's first book of poems, published while he was still an undergraduate, might be called "Asps and Lutes." It would be nostalgic for a life that never was. It would be world-weary. (He once saw the world, out of a train carriage window: it looked unreal.) It would be a carefully garish mixture, a cunningly evocative pudding full of plums pulled from the Sitwells and others, a mildly cacophonous hothouse of exotic horticultural and comic-erotic bric-a-brac, from which I extract these typical lines:—

> A cornucopia of phalluses
> Cascade on the vermilion palaces
> In arabesques and syrup rigadoons;
> Quince-breasted Circes of the zenanas
> Do catch this rain of cherry-wigged bananas
> And saraband beneath the raspberry moons.

After a tiff with the University authorities he vanishes into the Key of Blue—a made man.

If it were in the thirties, the title of his book might well be "Pharos, I Warn," and would consist of one of two kinds of verse. Either it would be made of long, lax, lackadaisical rhythms, dying falls, and images of social awareness:—

After the incessant means-test of the conspiratorial winter
Scrutinizing the tragic history of each robbed branch,
Look! the triumphant bourgeoning! spring
   gay as a workers' procession
To the newly-opened gymnasium!
Look! the full employment of the blossoms!

Or it would be daringly full of slang and street phrases, snippets
of song hits, Kipling jingles, kippered blues:—

We're sitting pretty
In the appalling city—
I know where we're going but I don't know where from—
Take it from me, boy,
You're my cup-of-tea-boy,
We're sitting on a big black bomb.

   Social awareness! That was the motto. He would talk over
coffee—("Adrian makes the best coffee in the whole of this un-
civilized island." "Tell me, Rodney, where *do* you get these
delicious little pink cakes?" "It's a secret!" "Oh, *do* tell. And I'll
give you that special receipt that Basil's Colonel brought back
from Ceylon, it takes three pounds of butter and a mango pod")
—of spending the long vacation in "somewhere *really* alive. I
mean, but really. Like the Rhondda Valley or something. I mean,
I know I'll feel really *orientated* there. I mean, one's so stagnant
here. Books, books. It's people that count. I mean, one's got to
know the miners." And he spends the long vacation with Reggie,
in Bonn. A volume of politico-travel chat follows, the promise
of which is amply fulfilled when, years later, he turns up as
Literary Secretary of I.A.C.T.—(International Arts Council Tomorrow).
   If Cedric were writing in the forties, he would, perhaps, be
engulfed, so that he could not see the wool for the Treece, in a
kind of "apocalyptic" batter, and his first volume might be entitled "Plangent Macrocosm," or "Heliogabalus in Pentecost."
Cedric can mix his metaphor, bog his cliché, and soak his stolen
symbols in stale ass's milk as glibly and glueily as the best of them.
   Next, London and reviewing. Reviewing, obviously, the work
of other poets. This, to do badly, is simple and, though not at
once, financially rewarding. The vocabulary that a conscientiously

dishonest reviewer of contemporary verse must learn is limited. Trend, of course, and impact, sphere of influence, Audenesque, the later Yeats, constructivism, schematic, ingeniously sprinkled, will help along, no end, the short and sweeping dismissal of the lifework of any adult and responsible poet.

The principal rules are few to remember: When reviewing, say, two entirely dissimilar books of verse, pit one against the other as though they were originally written in strict competition. "After Mr. A's subtle, taut, and integrated poetical comments or near-epigrams, Mr. B's long and sonorous heroic narrative, for all its textural richness and vibrative orchestration, rings curiously hollow" is an example of this most worth-while and labor-saving device. Decide, quite carefully, to be a staunch admirer of one particular poet, whether you like his poetry or not; cash in on him; make him your own; patent him; carve a niche with him. Bring his name, gratuitously, into your reviews: "Mr. E is, unfortunately, a poet much given to rhodomontade (unlike Hector Whistle)." "Reading Mr. D's admirably scholarly though, in places, pedestrian translations, we find ourselves longing for the cool ardor and consummate craftsmanship of Hector Whistle." Be careful, when you choose your poet, not to poach. Ask yourself first, "Is Hector Whistle anyone else's pigeon?"

Read all other reviews of the books you are about to review before you say a word yourself. Quote from the poems only when pressed for time: a review should be about the reviewer, not the poet. Be careful not to slate a bad rich poet unless he is notoriously mean, dead, or in America, for it is not such a long step from reviewing verse to editing a magazine, and the rich bad poet may well put up the money.

Returning to Cedric, let us suppose that he has, as a result of comparing a rich young man's verse with Auden's, to the detriment of Auden's, been given the editorship of a new literary periodical. (He may also be given a flat. If not, he should insist that the new periodical must have commodious offices. He then lives in them.) Cedric's first problem is what to call the thing. This is not easy, as most of the names that mean nothing at all—essential to the success of a new project—have all been used: *Horizon, Polemic, Harvest, Caravel, Seed, Transition, Arena, Circus, Cronos, Signposts, Wind and Rain*—they've all been had. Can you hear Cedric's mind churning away? "Vacuum," "Volcano," "Limbo," "Milestone," "Need," "Eruption," "Schism," "Data," "Arson." Yes, he's got it: "Chiaroscuro." The rest is easy: just the editing.

But let us look, very quickly, at some other methods of making poetry a going concern.

The Provincial Rush, or the Up-Rimbaud-and-At-Em approach. This is not wholeheartedly to be recommended as certain qualifications are essential. Before you swoop and burst upon the center of literary activity—which means, when you are very young, the right pubs, and, later, the right flats, and, later still, the right clubs—you must have behind you a body (it need have no head) of ferocious and un-understandable verse. (It is not, as I said before, my function to describe how these gauche and verbose ecstasies are achieved. Hart Crane found that, while listening, drunk, to Sibelius, he could turn out the stuff like billyho. A friend of mine, who has been suffering from a violent headache since he was eight, finds it so easy to write anyway he has to tie knots in his unpleasant handkerchief to remind him to stop. There are many methods, and always, when there's a will and slight delirium, there's a way.) Again, this poet must possess a thirst and constitution like that of a salt-eating pony, a hippo's hide, boundless energy, prodigious conceit, no scruples, and—most important of all, this can never be overestimated—a home to go *back* to in the provinces whenever he breaks down.

Of the poet who merely writes because he wants to write, who does not deeply mind if he is published or not, and who can put up with poverty and total lack of recognition in his lifetime, nothing of any pertinent value can be said. He is no businessman. Posterity Does Not Pay.

Also, and highly *un*recommended, are the following:—

The writing of limericks. Vast market, little or no pay.

Poems in crackers. Too seasonal.

Poems for children. This will kill you, and the children.

Obituaries in verse. Only established favorites used.

Poetry as a method of blackmail (by boring). Dangerous. The one you blackmail might retaliate by reading you aloud his unfinished tragedy about St. Bernard: "The Flask."

And lastly: *Poems on lavatory walls.* The reward is purely psychological.

(*1950*)

HOW TO BEGIN A STORY

The way to begin a story depends not so much upon what you mean by a story as upon the story itself and the public for which it is intended. That this goes without saying, need in no way deter me from saying it: these are notes in the margin of a never-to-be-written treatise and are free as the London air, though not so smutty.

It would, for example, be wrong, however pleasant, to begin a story for *Little Tim's Weekly* in the style of a sentimentally savage, gauchely cynical, American underworld novel salted with sex-slang, peppered with lead, sugared with stiffs, and stiff with cigars and sugars: the kind of novel beneath whose hard and sinister shell lurks no embryonic bird of prey, great Chicago auk or fabulous Brooklyn roc, but a backward, shy, and shabby backwood sparrow twittering for crumbs and buddies. Those flash, brash, cigar-mashing floozie-flayers and anti-social bad babies who, in recent gangster-films, confess, at some Ufa-lighted moment in abattoir, railway-siding, or condemned cell, that they have always been kinda unwanted and lonesome, even back in mid-western little Bloodville, and that it all began when their dipsomaniac second stepmothers put them on the fire for saying their prayers—these psychopathic gorillas coked to the gills have no place in Little Tim's cosmography, however much Little Tim would appreciate it, and the writer of children's stories should never, in any circumstances, emotional or atomic, begin with an expletive-packed and monosyllabic description of a raid by the vice-squad on a clip-joint for retired rod-men. It is legitimate to begin a children's story with a conversation between rats; but only between certain kinds of rats.

Neither should the writer of a story intended to command a steady, unsensational provincial sale, and concerning the birth, education, financial ups and downs, marriage, separations and deaths of five generations of a family of Lancashire cotton-weavers, begin with, say, the Joyceian interior monologue of a moronic haberdasher trapped in a lift full of moths, or with a twee scene, in Hopskipandjump Town or Eiderdown Land, between Gruffums, the Lion, and Hold, that Tiger.

The man who begins a story for a girl's popular weekly—*Myrtle's* or *Pam's,* or maybe it is *Greta's* now, or *Ingrid's*—with a subtle analysis of the state of mind of a neurotic young man of letters about to meet a phobia, socially, in a disused Nissen hut, will never make the grade and is doomed to perpetual immurement in magazines with a circulation of seventeen poets and a woman who once met Kafka's aunt.

Now let us consider, most briefly, just a very few of the many favourite ways of beginning stories, and see if we can put a little new life into them.

School stories first: not the dull ones about the repressions and urges of sensitive plants and backward sons, and the first dawning of love and Shelley on the awakening mind, but the good, or bad, old stories which are all about tea and muffins in the cosy study, midnight spreads by candlelight in the ill-patrolled dormitory, escapes by knotted sheets to out-of-bound circuses or fairs, the ruthless ragging and baiting of unpopular masters and impecunious buffoons, the expulsion of cads for smoking in the fives-court—poor little sallow Maltravers with the dark rings already under his roué's eyes—and all the trivial tribal warfares of fantastic and ageless boys. The onomatopœic, gemmed and magnetic, time-honoured opening cannot be bettered:

> "Leggo!"
> "Geroff!"
> "Yaroo!"

And then, of course:

"These stentorian cries echoed down the corridor of the Upper Shell."

The novice should begin every school story with exactly those words.

In the next sentence he must introduce his principal characters, a bunch of bold, breathless, exclamatory, ink-stained, beastly, Dickensian-surnamed boys with their caps awry, their lines undone, pets in their desks, paper-pellets in their pockets, and barbarous though innocuous oaths on their unrazored lips. But let us introduce a new element:

"Leggo!"
"Geroff!"
"Yaroo!"

"These stentorian cries echoed down the corridor of the Upper Shell as Tom Happy and his inseparables, known to all Owlhurst as the 'Filthy Five,' lurched arm-in-arm out of Mrs. Motherwell's fully licensed tuckshop."

There you have a beginning at once conventional and startling. The reader is at your mercy. And you can continue, within the accepted framework and using only the loudest, minutest, and most formal vocabulary, to describe such goings on as the formation, by Tom Happy, of the Owlhurst Suicide Club and the setting up of a hookah in the boothole.

Then there is the story of rural life. I don't mean the depressing tale, told through four interminable seasons, of rugged toil and weather-beaten love on an isolated farm of that part of Sussex where you can't hear the thrushes for the noise of typewriters; nor the earthy, middenish record, stuffed with nature lore and agricultural information, studded—if that is the word—with all too precise observations of animal behaviour, whiskered with "characters," riddled with unintelligible snatches of folk verse and altogether jocular as a boot, of how a middle-aged literary man "discovered" the country and his soul, price eight and six.

No; I mean the kind of story set in a small, lunatic area of Wessex, full of saintly or reprehensible vicars, wanton maidens, biblical sextons, and old men called Parsnip or Dottle. Let us imagine a typical beginning:

"Mr. Beetroot stood on a hill overlooking the village of Upper Story. He saw that there was something wrong in it. Mr. Beetroot was a retired mole-trapper. He had retired because he had trapped all the moles. It was a fine winter's morning, and there were little clouds in the sky like molehills. Mr. Beetroot caught a rabbit, taught it the alphabet, let it go, and walked slowly down the hill."

There we have firmly fixed the location and mood of the story, and have become well, if briefly, acquainted with Mr. Beetroot, a lover of animals and addicted to animal education.

The common reader—legendary cretin—now knows what is coming to him: Mr. Beetroot, that cracked though cosmic symbol of something or other, will, in the nutty village, with dialect, oafs and potted sermons, conduct his investigation into unreal rural life. Everyone in this sophisticatedly contrived bucolic morality has his or her obsession: Minnie Wurzel wants only the vicar; the vicar, the Reverend Nut, wants only the ghost of William Cowper to come into his brown study and read him *The Task*; the Sexton wants worms; worms want the vicar. Lambkins, on these impossible hills, frolic, gambol, and are sheepish under the all-seeing eye of Uncle Teapot, the Celestial Tinker. Cruel farmers persecute old cowherds called Crumpet, who talk, all day long, to cows; cows, tired of vaccine-talk in which they can have no part, gore, in a female manner, the aged relatives of cruel farmers; it is all very cosy in Upper Story. But so the reader—cretinous legend —thinks.

The beginner, beginning a story of this kind, would be wise to . . .

I see there is little, or no, time to continue my instructional essay on "How To Begin a Story." "How To End a Story" is, of course, a different matter. . . . *One* way of ending a story is . . .

(1946)

THE FESTIVAL EXHIBITION 1951

The extent of the site of the Exhibition on the South Bank of the Thames in the heart of London is four and a half acres. There are twenty-two pavilions in the Exhibition, and thirteen restaurants, cafés, bars and buffets.

Some people visit the twenty-two pavilions first, then glazed and crippled, windless, rudderless, and a little out of their minds, teeter, weeping, to one of the thirteen restaurants, cafés, bars and buffets to find it packed to the dazzlingly painted and, possibly, levitating doors.

Other people visit all thirteen restaurants, cafés, bars and buffets before attacking a pavilion, and rarely get further than the Dome of Discovery, which they find confusing, full, as it is, of totem poles, real dogs in snow, locusts, stars, the sun, the moon, things bubbling, thunder and lightning machines, chemical and physical surprises. And some never return.

Most people who wish, at the beginning, anyway, to make sense of the Exhibition, follow the course indicated in the official Guidebook—a series of conflicting arrows which lead many visitors who cannot understand these things slapsplash into the Thames— and work their way dutifully right through the land of Britain, the glaciers of twenty thousand years ago, and the inferno of blown desert sand which is now Birmingham, out at last into the Pavilion of Health—where, perhaps, they stop for an envious moment at the sign that says "Euthanasia"—and on to the netted and capstaned, bollarded, buoyed, seashelled, pebbly beautiful seaside of summer childhood gone.

And other visitors begin, of course, at the end. They are the people without whom the Exhibition could not exist, nor the country it trombones and floats in with its lions and unicorns made of ears of wheat, its birds that sing to the push of a button, its flaming water and its raspberry fountains. They are the suspicious people over whose eyes no coloured Festival wool can possibly be pulled, the great undiddleable; they are the women who "will not queue on any account" and who smuggle in dyspeptic dogs; the strangely calculating men who think that the last pavilion must be first because it is number twenty-two; the people who believe they are somewhere else, and never find out they are not; sharp people who have been there before, who know the ropes, who chuckle to their country cousins, "You get double your money's worth this way"; vaguely persecuted people, always losing their gloves, who know that the only way they could *ever* get around would be to begin at the end, which they do not want to; people of militant individuality who proclaim their right, as Englishmen, to look at the damfool place however they willy-nilly will; people nervously affected by all such occasions, who want to know only, "where's the place?"; timid people who want to be as far from the Skylon as possible, because 'you never know"; foreigners, who have been directed this way by a school of irresponsible wits; glassy benighted men who are trying to remember they must see something of the Exhibition to remember before they go home and try to describe it to their families; young people, hand-in-love, who will giggle at whatever they see, at a goldfish in a pond, a model of the *Queen Elizabeth*, or a flint hammer; people too bored to yawn, long and rich as borzois, who, before they have seen it, have seen better shows in Copenhagen and San Francisco; eccentric people: men with their deerstalker caps tied with rope to their lapels, who carry dried nut sandwiches and little containers of yoghourt in hairy green knapsacks labelled "glass with care"; fat, flustered women in as many layers of coats as an onion or a cabdriver, hunting in a fever through fifty fluffed pockets to find a lost packet of birdseed they are going to give to the parrots who are not there; old scaly sneezing men, born of lizards in a snuff-bin, who read, wherever they go, from books in tiny print, and who never look up, even at the tureen-lid of the just-tethered dome on the shining Skylon, the sky-going nylon, the cylindrical leg-of-the-future jetting, almost, to the exhibition of stars; *real* eccentrics: people who have come to the South Bank to study the growth and development of Britain from the Iron Age till now.

Here they will find no braying pageantry, no taxidermal museum of Culture, no cold and echoing inhuman hygienic barracks of technical information, no shoddily cajoling emporium of tasteless Empire wares; but something very odd indeed, magical and parochial: a parish pump made of flying glass and thistledown gauze-thin steel, a rolypoly pudding full of luminous, melodious bells, wheels, coils, engines and organs, alembics and jorums in a palace in thunderland sizzling with scientific witches' brews, a place of trains, bones, planes, ships, sheep, shapes, snipe, mobiles, marble, brass bands and cheese, a place painted regardless, and by hand.

Perhaps you'll think I'm shovelling the colour on too thickly, that I am, as it were, speaking under the influence of strong pink. (And what a lot of pink—rose, raspberry, strawberry, peach, flesh, blush, lobster, salmon, tallyho—there is, plastered and doodled all over this four-acre gay and soon-to-be-gone Festival City in sprawling London.) London: to many of us who live in the country, the Capital punishment. Perhaps you will go on a cool, dull day, sane as a biscuit, and find that the Exhibition does, indeed, tell the story "of British contributions to world civilisation in the arts of peace"; that, and nothing else. But I'm pleased to doubt it. Of *course* it is instructive; of *course* there is behind it an articulate and comprehensive plan; it can show you, unless you are an expert, more about, say, mineralogy or the ionosphere than you may want to know. It's bursting its buttons, in an orderly manner, with knowledge. But what everyone I know, and have observed, seems to like most in it is the gay, absurd, irrelevant, delighting imagination that flies and booms and spurts and trickles out of the whole bright boiling; the small stone oddity that squints at you round a sharp, daubed corner; the sexless abstract sculptures serenely and secretly existing out of time in old cold worlds of their own in places that appear, but only for one struck second, inappropriate; the linked terra-cotta man and woman fly-defying gravity and elegantly hurrying up a w.c. wall; the sudden design of hands on another wall, as though the painter had said, "Oh, to the daft devil with what I'm doing," and just slap-slap-slapped all over the ochre his spread-out fingers and thumbs, ten blunt arrows, or as though large convict-birds, if there are any such, had waddled up the wall and webbed it as they went. You see people go along briskly down the wide white avenues towards the pavilion of their fancy—"Our Humbert's dead keen on seeing the milk separators" —and suddenly stop: another fancy swings or bubbles in front of his eyes. What is it they see? Indigo water waltzing to music. Row after row of rosy rolling balls spread on tall screens like the counting-beads of Wellsian children fed on the Food of the

Gods. Sheets of asbestos tied on to nowhere, by nothing, for nothing is anchored here and at the clap of hands the whole gallimaufry could take off to Sousa and zoom up the flagged sky. Small child book-painted mobiles along the bridges that, at a flick of wind, become windmills and thrum round at night like rainbows with arms. Or the steel-and-platinum figure—created by the Welsh engineer and architect, Richard Huws—of maybe a merwoman standing, if that is the word for one who grows out of it, in arc-light water; she weeps as she is wept on; first her glinting breast, then another plane of her, tips, slides, shoots, shelves, swings and sidles out to take, from the lake of her birth, one ton of water at a time to Handel's *Water Music*, absorbs it, inhales it through dripping steel, then casts and cascades it off and out again. Or even the hundreds of little vivid steel chairs that look like hundreds of little vivid steel people sitting down.

In the pavilion called "The Natural Scene," see the seals and eagles, the foxes and wild cats, of these still wild islands, and the natural history of owled and cuckooed, ottered, unlikely London. A great naked tree climbs in the middle of all, with prodigious butterflies and beetles on it. A blackbird lights up, and the aviary's full of his singing; a thrush, a curlew, a skylark.

And, in the "Country," see all the sculpted and woven loaves, in the shape of sheaves of wheat, in curls, plaits, and whirls. And men are thatching the roofs of cottages; and—what could be more natural?—the men are made of straw. And what a pleasure of baskets! Trugs, creels, pottles and punnets, hoppers, dorsers and mounds, wiskets and whiskets. And if these are not the proper words, they should be.

In "The Lion and the Unicorn" is celebrated, under flights of birds, the "British Character," that stubborn, stupid, seabound, lyrical, paradoxical dark farrago of uppishness, derring-do, and midsummer moonshine all fluting, snug, and copper-bottomed. Justice, for some reason, looms in the midst of the hall, its two big wigs back to back, its black and scarlet robes falling below. The body of Justice is shelves of lawbooks. The black spaces beneath the white wigs look like the profiles of eagles. The white knight rides there too, too much a Don Quixote for my looking-glass land, and very potless and panless. A bravoo-ing hand pats his plaster back, and tells him good night. There is a machine for, I believe, grinding smoke. And a tea set, I failed to see, of salmon bones. But, in all this authentically eccentric Exhibition, it is the Eccentrics' Corner that is the most insipid. Some of the dullest exhibits in the pavilion are relieved by surrounding extravagance; but the department devoted to the rhapsodic inspirations of extravagance is by far the dullest. Why was not the exquisite talent utilised of the warlock who, offering his services to the Festival authorities, assured them he would, to order, throw a rainbow over the Thames? I wish he would throw a rainbow over me as I walk through the grey days. "Yes, we can tell it's him coming," the envious neighbours would murmur, "we recognise his rainbow." And, on the balcony, there is a row of tiny theatres; in each, the stage is set for a Shakespearean play; and out of the theatres come the words of the players. If you're in luck, something may go wrong with the works and Hamlet rant from Dunsinane.

In "Homes and Gardens," blink at the grievous furniture, ugly as sin and less comfy.

In the "Transport Pavilions," goggle at the wizard diesels and the smashing, unpuffing streamlines and the miracle model railway for dwarf nabobs.

Then, if there are by this time no spots in front of your eyes, go to the Telecinema and see them astonishingly all around you: spots with scarlet tadpole tails, and spottedly sinuous tin tacks dancing with dissolving zebra heads, and blobs and nubbins and rubbery squirls receding, to zigzag, blasts of brass down nasty polychrome corridors, a St. Vitus's gala of abstract shapes and shades in a St. Swithin's day of torrential dazzling darning needles. Sit still in the startling cinema and be kissed by a giraffe, who stretches his neck right out of the screen for you. Follow the deliberately coloured course of the Thames, the Royal River; the whispering water's more like water than water ever was; closer, closer, comes the slow kingfisher—blue water and suddenly it ripples all over you: that'll be the day when film stars do the same.

Go to the South Bank first by day; the rest of your times at night. Sit at a café table in the night of musical lights, by the radiant river, the glittering Skylon above you rearing to be off, the lit pavilion, white, black and silver in sweeps of stone and feathery steel, transplendent round you as you sip and think:

This is the first time I have ever truly seen that London

whose sweet Thames runs softly, that minstrel mermaid of a town, the water-streeted eight-million-headed village in a blaze. *This* is London, not the huge petty misshaped nightmare I used to know as I humdrummed along its graceless streets through fog and smoke and past the anonymous unhappy bodies lively as wet brollies. This Festival is London. The arches of the bridges leap into light; the moon clocks glow; the river sings; the harmonious pavilions are happy. And this is what London should always be like, till St. Paul's falls down and the sea slides over the Strand.

(1951)

THE INTERNATIONAL EISTEDDFOD

Llangollen. A town in a vale in rolling green North Wales on a windy July morning. The sun squints out and is puffed back again into the grey clouds blowing, full to the ragged rims with rain, across the Berwyn Hills. The white-horsed river Dee hisses and paws over the hills of its stones and under the grey-beard bridge. Wind smacks the river and you; it's a cold, cracking morning; birds hang and rasp over the whipped river, against their will, as though frozen still, or are wind-chaffed and scattered towards the gusty trees. As you drift down Castle Street with your hair flying, or your hat or umbrella dancing to be off and take the sky, you see and hear all about you the decorous, soberly dressed and headgeared, silent and unsmiling inhabitants of the tame town. You could be in any Welsh town on any windy snip of a morning, with only the birds and the river fuming and the only brightness the numberless greens and high purple of the hills. Everything is very ordinary in Llangollen; everything is nicely dull, except the summer world of wind and feathers, leaves and water. There is, if you are deaf, blind, and dumb, with a heart like cold bread pudding, nothing to remark or surprise. But rub your eyes with your black gloves. Here, over the bridge, come three Javanese, winged, breastplated, helmeted, carrying gongs and steel bubbles. Kilted, sporraned, tartan'd, daggered Scotsmen reel and strathspey up a side-street, piping hot. Burgundian girls, wearing, on their heads, bird cages made of velvet, suddenly whisk on the pavement into a coloured dance. A Viking goes into a pub. In black felt feathered hats and short leather trousers, enormous Austrians, with thighs big as Welshmen's bodies, but much browner, yodel to fiddles and split the rain with their smiles. Frilled, ribboned, sashed, fezzed and white-turbaned, in baggy-blue sharavári and squashed red boots, Ukrainians with Manchester accents gopak up the hill.

Everything is strange in Llangollen. You wish you had a scarlet hat, and bangles, and a little bagpipe to call your own, but it does not matter. The slapping bell-dancers, the shepherds and chamois-hunters, the fiddlers and fluters, the players on gongs and mandolins, guitars, harps and trumpets, the beautiful flashing boys and girls of a score and more of singing countries, all the colours of the international rainbow, do not mind at all your mouse-brown moving among them: though you long, all the long Eisteddfod week, for a cloak like a blue sea or a bonfire to sweep and blaze in the wind, and a cap of bells, and a revelling waistcoat, and a great alphorn to blow all over Wales from the ruins of Dinas Brân.

Now follow your nose, and the noise of guitars, and the flying hues and flourish of those big singing-birds in their clogs and aprons and bonnets, veils, flowers, more flowers, and lace, past the wee shoppes, through the babel of the bridge, by the very white policeman conducting from a rostrum, and up the tide of the hill, past popcorn and raspberryade, to the tented Field.

Green, packed banks run, swarming, down to the huge marquee there that groans and strains and sings in the sudden squalls like an airship crewed full of choirs. Music spills out of the microphones all over the humming field. Out of the wind-tugged tent it rises in one voice, and the crowd outside is hushed away into Spain. In a far corner of the field, young men and women begin to dance, for every reason in the world. Out skims the sun from a cloud-shoal. The spaniel ears of the little tents flap. Children collect the autographs of Dutch farmers. You hear a hive of summer hornets: it is the Burgundian *vielle*, a mandolin with a handle. Palestrina praises from Bologna to the choral picnickers. A Breton holiday sings in the wind, to clog-tramp and *biniou*.

Here they come, to this cup and echo of hills, people who love to make music, from France, Ireland, Norway, Italy, Switzerland, Spain, Java and Wales: fine singers and faulty, nimble dancers and rusty, pipers to make the dead swirl or chanters with crows in their throats: all countries, shapes, ages, and colours, sword-dancers, court-dancers, cross-dancers, clog-dancers, dale-dancers, morris, coilidhe, and highland bolero, flamenco heel-and-toe. They love to make music move. What a rush of dancing to Llangollen's feet! And, oh, the hubbub of tongues and toes in the dark chapels where every morning there's such a shining noise as you'd think would drive the Sunday bogles out of their doldrums for ever and ever.

Inside the vast marquee that drags at its anchors, eight thousand people—and you—face a sea of flowers, begonias, magnolias, lupines, lobelias, grown for these dancing days in the gardens of the town. Banks and waves of plants and flowers flow to the stage where a company from Holland—eight married pairs of them, the oldest in the late fifties, the youngest twenty or so—are performing, in sombre black, a country dance called, "Throw Your Wife Away." This is followed, appropriately and a little later, by a dance called, "You Can't Catch Me." The movements of the humorous and simple dance are gay and sprightly. The men of the company dance like sad British railway-drivers in white clogs. Under their black, peaked caps, their faces are stern, weather-scored, and unrelenting. The quicker the music, the gloomier they clap and clog on the invisible cobbles of cold clean kitchens. The frenzied flute and fiddle whip them up into jet-black bliss as they frolic like undertakers. Long Dutch winter nights envelop them. Brueghel has painted them. They are sober as potatoes. Their lips move as they stamp and bow. Perhaps they are singing. Certainly, they are extremely happy.

And Austrians, then, to fiddles and guitar, sing a song of mowers in the Alpine meadows. Sworded Ukrainians—I mean, Ukrainians with swords—leap and kick above the planted sea. People from Tournas, in the Burgundy country, dance to accordion and *cabrette*, the Dance of the Vine-Dressers after Harvest. They plant the vines, put the leaves on the branches, hang up the grapes, pick the grapes, and press the wine. "God gave us wine," they sing as they dance, and the wine is poured into glasses and the dancers drink. (But the wine's not as real as the pussyfoot nudge and shudder down the aisles.)

All day, the music goes on. Bell-padded, bald-ricked, and braided, these other foreigners, the English, dance fiercely out of the past; and some have beards, spade, gold, white, and black, to dance and wag as well.

And a chorus of Spanish ladies are sonorous and beautiful in their nighties.

And little girls from Obernkirchen sing like pigtailed angels.

All day the song and dancing in this transformed valley, this green cup of countries in the country of Wales, goes on until the sun goes in. Then, in the ship of the tent, under the wind-filled sails, watchers and listeners grow slow and close into one cloud of shadow; they gaze, from their deep lulled dark, on to the lighted deck where the country dancers weave in shifting-coloured harvests of light.

And then you climb down hill again, in a tired tide, and over the floodlit Dee to the town that won't sleep for a whole melodious week or, if it does at all, will hear all night in its sleep the hills fiddle and strum and the streets painted with tunes.

The bars are open as though they could not shut and Sunday never come down over the fluting town like a fog or a shutter. For every reason in the world, there's a wave of dancing in the main, loud street. A fiddle at a corner tells you to dance and you do in the moon though you can't dance a step for all the Ukrainians in Llangollen. Peace plays on a concertina in the vigorous, starry street, and nobody is surprised.

When you leave the last voices and measures of the sweet-throated, waltzing streets, the lilt and ripple of the Dee leaping, and the light of the night, to lie down, and the strewn town lies down to sleep in its hills and ring of echoes, you will remember that nobody was surprised at the turn the town took and the life it danced for one week of the long, little year. The town sang and danced, as though it were right and proper as the rainbow or the rare sun to celebrate the old bright turning earth and its bullied people. Are you surprised that people still can dance and sing in a world on its head? The only surprising thing about miracles, however small, is that they sometimes happen.

(1953)

A VISIT TO AMERICA

Across the United States of America, from New York to California and back, glazed, again, for many months of the year, there streams and sings for its heady supper a dazed and prejudiced procession of European lecturers, scholars, sociologists, economists, writers, authorities on this and that and even, in theory, on the United States of America. And, breathlessly, between addresses and receptions, in planes and trains and boiling hotel bedroom ovens, many of these attempt to keep journals and diaries.

At first, confused and shocked by shameless profusion and almost shamed by generosity, unaccustomed to such importance as they are assumed, by their hosts, to possess, and up against the barrier of a common language, they write in their notebooks like demons, generalising away, on character and culture and the American political scene. But, towards the middle of their middle-aged whisk through middle-western clubs and universities, the fury of the writing flags; their spirits are lowered by the spirit with which they are everywhere strongly greeted and which, in ever increasing doses, they themselves lower; and they begin to mistrust themselves, and their reputations—for they have found, too often, that an audience will receive a lantern-lecture on, say, Ceramics, with the same uninhibited enthusiasm that it accorded the very week before to a paper on the Modern Turkish Novel. And, in their diaries, more and more do such entries appear as, "No way of escape!" or "Buffalo!" or "I am beaten," until at last they cannot write a word. And, twittering all over, old before their time, with eyes like rissoles in the sand, they are helped up the gangway of the home-bound liner by kind bosom friends (of all kinds and bosoms) who boister them on the back, pick them up again, thrust bottles, sonnets, cigars, addresses, into their pockets, have a farewell party in their cabin, pick them up again, and, snickering and yelping, are gone: to wait at the dockside for another boat from Europe and another batch of fresh, green lecturers.

There they go, every spring, from New York to Los Angeles: exhibitionists, polemicists, histrionic publicists, theological rhetoricians, historical hoddy-doddies, balletomanes, ulterior decorators, windbags and bigwigs and humbugs, men in love with stamps, men in love with steaks, men after millionaires' widows, men with elephantiasis of the reputation (huge trunks and teeny minds), authorities on gas, bishops, best-sellers, editors looking for writers, writers looking for publishers, publishers looking for dollars, existentialists, serious physicists with nuclear missions, men from the B.B.C. who speak as though they had the Elgin marbles in their mouths, potboiling philosophers, professional Irishmen (very lepri-corny), and, I am afraid, fat poems with slim volumes.

And see, too, in that linguacious stream, the tall monocled men, smelling of saddle soap and club armchairs, their breath a nice blending of whiskey and fox's blood, with big protruding upper-class tusks and country mustaches, presumably invented in England and sent abroad to advertise *Punch,* who lecture to women's clubs on such unlikely subjects as "The History of Etching in the Shetland Islands"; and the brassy-bossy menwomen, with corrugated-iron perms, and hippo hides, who come, self-announced, as "ordinary British housewives," to talk to rich minked chunks of American matronhood about the iniquity of the Health Services, the criminal sloth of the miners, the *visible* tail and horns of Mr. Aneurin Bevan, and the fear of everyone in England to go out alone at night because of the organised legions of coshboys against whom the police are powerless owing to the refusal of those in power to equip them with revolvers and to flog to ribbons every adolescent offender on any charge at all.

And there shiver and teeter also, meek and driven, those British authors unfortunate enough to have written, after years of unadventurous forgotten work, one bad novel which became enormously popular on both sides of the Atlantic. At home, when success first hit them, they were mildly delighted; a couple of literary luncheons went sugar-tipsy to their heads, like the washing sherry served before those luncheons; and perhaps, as the lovely money rolled lushly in, they began to dream, in their moony writers' way, of being able to retire to the county, keep wasps (or was it bees?) and never write another lousy word. But in come the literary agent's triggermen and the publisher's armed narks: "You must go to the States and make a Personal Appearance.

Your novel is *killing* them over there, and we're not surprised either. You must go round the States lecturing to women." And the inoffensive writers, who have never dared lecture anyone, let alone women—they are frightened of women, they do not understand them, women, they write about women as creatures that never existed, and the women lap it up—these sensitive plants cry out, "But what shall we lecture about?"

"The English Novel."

"I don't read novels."

"Great Women in Fiction."

"I don't like fiction *or* women."

But off they are wafted, first class, in the plush bowels of the *Queen Victoria,* with a list of engagements long as a New York menu or a half-hour with a book by Charles Morgan, and soon they are losing their little cold-as-goldfish paw in the great general glutinous handshake of a clutch of enveloping hostesses.

I think, by the way, that it was Ernest Raymond, the author of *Tell England,* who once made a journey round the American women's clubs, being housed and entertained at each small town he stopped at, by the richest and largest and furriest lady available. On one occasion he stopped at some little station and was met, as usual, by an enormous motor-car full of a large horn-rimmed businessman—looking exactly like a large horn-rimmed businessman on the films—and his roly-poly pearly wife. Mr. Raymond sat with her in the back of the car, and off they went, the husband driving. At once, she began to say how utterly delighted she and her husband and the committee were to have him at their Women's Literary and Social Guide, and to compliment him on his books.

"I don't think I've ever, in all my life, enjoyed a book so much as *Sorrel and Son,*" she said. "What you don't know about human nature! I think Sorrel is one of the most beautiful characters ever portrayed."

Ernest Raymond let her talk on, while he stared, embarrassed, in front of him. All he could see were the double chins that her husband wore at the back of his neck. On and on she gushed in praise of *Sorrel and Son* until he could stand it no longer.

"I quite agree with you," he said. "A beautiful book indeed. But I'm afraid I didn't write *Sorrel and Son*. It was written by an old friend of mine, Mr. Warwick Deeping."

And the large horn-rimmed double-chinned husband at the wheel said, without turning: "Caught again, Emily."

See the garrulous others, also, gabbing and garlanded from one nest of culture-vultures to another: people selling the English way of life and condemning the American way as they swig and guzzle through it; people resurrecting the theories of surrealism for the benefit of remote parochial female audiences who did not know it was dead, not having ever known it had been alive; people talking about Etruscan pots and pans to a bunch of dead pans and wealthy pots in Boston. And there, too, in the sticky thick of lecturers moving across the continent black with clubs, go the foreign poets, catarrhal troubadours, lyrical one-night-standers, dollar-mad nightingales, remittance-bards from at home, myself among them booming with the worst.

Did we pass one another, en route, all unknowing, I wonder; one of us spry-eyed, with clean, white lectures and a soul he could call his own, going buoyantly west to his remunerative doom in the great state university factories; another returning dog-eared as his clutch of poems and his carefully typed impromptu asides? I ache for us both. There one goes, unsullied as yet, in his Pullman pride, toying—oh boy!—with a blunderbuss bourbon, being smoked by a large cigar, riding out to the wide-open spaces of the faces of his waiting audience. He carries, besides his literary baggage, a new, dynamic razor, just on the market, bought in New York, which operates at the flick of a thumb, but cuts the thumb to the bone; a tin of new shaving-lather which is worked with the other, unbleeding, thumb, and covers not only the face but the whole bathroom and, instantly freezing, makes an arctic, icicled cave from which it takes two sneering bellboys to extract him; and, of course, a nylon shirt. This, he dearly believes, from the advertisements, he can himself wash in his hotel, hang to dry overnight, and put on, without ironing, in the morning. (In my case, no ironing was needed, for, as someone cruelly pointed out in print, I looked, anyway, like an unmade bed.)

He is vigorously welcomed at the station by an earnest crew-cut platoon of giant collegiates, all chasing the butterfly culture with net, notebook, poison bottle, pin and label, each with at least thirty-six terribly white teeth, and nursed away, as heavily gently as though he were an imbecile rich aunt with a short prospect of life, into a motor-car in which, for a mere fifty miles or so travelled at poet-breaking speed, he assures them of the correctness of their assumption that he is half-witted by stammering inconsequential answers in an over-British accent to their genial questions about what international conference Stephen Spender might be attending at the moment, or the reactions of British poets to the work of a famous American whose name he did not know or catch. He is then taken to a small party of only a few hundred people all of whom hold the belief that what a visiting lecturer needs before he trips on to the platform is just enough martinis so that he can trip off the platform as well. And, clutching his explosive glass, he is soon contemptuously dismissing, in a flush of ignorance and fluency, the poetry of those androgynous literary ladies with three names who produce a kind of verbal ectoplasm to order as a waiter dishes up spaghetti—only to find that the fiercest of these, a wealthy huntress of small, seedy lions (such as himself), who stalks the middle-western bush with ears and rifle cocked, is his hostess for the evening. Of the lecture, he remembers little but the applause and maybe two questions: "Is it true that the young English intellectuals are *really* psychological?" or, "I always carry Kierkegaard in my pocket. What do you carry?"

Late at night, in his room, he fills a page of his journal with a confused, but scathing, account of his first engagement; summarises American advanced education in a paragraph that will be meaningless tomorrow; and falls to sleep where he is immediately chased through long, dark thickets by a Mrs. Mabel Frankincense Mehaffey, with a tray of martinis and lyrics.

And there goes the other happy poet bedraggledly back to New York which struck him all of a sheepish never-sleeping heap at first, but which seems to him now, after the ulcerous rigours of a lecturer's spring, a haven cosy as toast, cool as an icebox, and safe as skyscrapers.

(*1953*)